# ALIGN the DESIGN

# ALIGN the DESIGN

## A Blueprint for School Improvement

Nancy J. Mooney ||| Ann T. Mausbach

Association for Supervision and Curriculum Development
Alexandria, Virginia USA

Association for Supervision and Curriculum Development
1703 N. Beauregard St. • Alexandria, VA 22311-1714 USA
Phone: 800-933-2723 or 703-578-9600 • Fax: 703-575-5400
Web site: www.ascd.org • E-mail: member@ascd.org
Author guidelines: www.ascd.org/write

Gene R. Carter, *Executive Director;* Nancy Modrak, *Publisher;* Julie Houtz, *Director of Book Editing & Production;* Leah Lakins, *Project Manager;* Greer Beeken, *Senior Graphic Designer;* Keith Demmons, *Typesetter;* Sarah Plumb, *Production Specialist*



All Web links in this book are correct as of the publication date below but may have become inactive or otherwise modified since that time. If you notice a deactivated or changed link, please e-mail books@ascd.org with the words "Link Update" in the subject line. In your message, please specify the Web link, the book title, and the page number on which the link appears.

PAPERBACK ISBN: 978-1-4166-0625-3 ASCD product #108005 s2/08
Also available as an e-book through ebrary, netLibrary, and many online booksellers (see Books in Print for the ISBNs).

Quantity discounts for the paperback edition only: 10–49 copies, 10%; 50+ copies, 15%; for 1,000 or more copies, call 800-933-2723, ext. 5634, or 703-575-5634. For desk copies: member@ascd.org.

**Library of Congress Cataloging-in-Publication Data**

Mooney, Nancy J.
Align the design : a blueprint for school improvement / Nancy Mooney and Ann Mausbach.
p. cm.
Includes bibliographical references and index.
ISBN 978-1-4166-0625-3 (pbk. : alk. paper) 1. School improvement programs--United States. 2. Academic achievement--United States. I. Mausbach, Ann. II. Title.

LB2822.82.M66 2008
371.200973

2007041371

18 17 16 15 14 13 12 11 10 09 08 1 2 3 4 5 6 7 8 9 10 11 12

# ALIGN the DESIGN

## A Blueprint for School Improvement

# Acknowledgments


## From Nancy

I acknowledge with deep gratitude the blessings of faith, family, and friends. The influence of each on my life and work is without measure.

Many educators contributed to and influenced the school improvement work discussed in this book. The central office administration of the St. Joseph School District in St. Joseph, Missouri, past and present, put a high priority on teaching and learning, and supported my part of the team's efforts to raise achievement and grow leaders. I treasure the friendship and contributions of my closest central office associates. The elementary and secondary principals in St. Joseph are the backbone of my work, and I am grateful beyond measure for their friendship and commitment to improving schools. Without the teachers in St. Joseph, none of this work would be possible, so I extend to them recognition for their dedication to teaching and willingness to make changes along the way.

During my years in the central office, Brenda Elifrits and Rhonda Hoselton served as administrative assistants. Many of the documents and professional development experiences that form the framework of this book would not have been completed without their able assistance. I am especially grateful to colleagues from districts outside of St. Joseph who have graciously embraced and contributed to the school improvement processes in this book, particularly Rita Fisher, Kevin Daniel, and my respected co-author and friend, Ann Mausbach. ASCD gave wonderful support from the beginning of this project through its completion. The staff, particularly Scott Willis and Leah Lakins, helped this book become a reality.

Finally, I acknowledge my family, who surround me with encouragement and hope. I owe deep gratitude to Frank and Marjorie Fletcher, who taught me to live by faith and value education. I thank Joel and Jennifer Mooney, Isabela, and Fina for the joy they bring to my life and their encouragement all along the way. Above all, I am forever grateful that I married Russ Mooney. His steady and unwavering support means everything. Without him, this book would be a dream never lived or written.

## From Ann

I would like to acknowledge several people who helped make this book a reality. First, I want to thank the "gang at the ERC." Their behind-the-scenes support, patience, and organizational skills allowed me to do the work outlined in this book. Thanks also go to the Liberty School District administrative team in Liberty, Missouri. These dedicated individuals understood that learning is the real mission of schooling and were always open to new ways to get the job done. Special thanks to Dr. W. Scott Taveau. His support and leadership gave me wings, and I will forever be indebted to him for that gift.

Most importantly, I would like to thank "my boys," my sons Jack and Mark, for their unending source of inspiration, and my husband Tim, for being my greatest fan. Their love, faith, and support have made all things possible in my life.

# Introduction

Many of you know how it feels to be on a diet and not be successful. You stick to your diet plan during the week, but you find yourself bingeing on the weekend or special occasions. After you successfully lose the weight, the minute you go off the diet, you gain all of the weight back and then some.

One of the major reasons that diets fail is that individuals don't do *all* the things that are necessary to lose weight. Successful dieters must look at all the principles that make weight loss attainable, such as setting goals, sticking to a realistic eating plan, exercising consistently, and joining a support group. A lack of attention to any of these processes will yield diminished results, dieter frustration, and, ultimately, abandoning the diet.

Diet failure also occurs because so many people view diets as a quick fix rather than a lifestyle change. Dieting can't be something that occurs five days a week and then thrown out the window whenever the mood strikes. Long-term, sustainable weight loss is a result of rethinking what and how you eat *and* increasing your daily physical activity. It has to be a lifetime commitment and a lifestyle change.

Why are we discussing diets in a book focused on school improvement and student achievement? The lessons learned from unsuccessful diets provide insight into why school improvement efforts for many schools and districts have failed. School improvement efforts can often feel like the latest diet fad. It is not uncommon to see school administrators implement programs that they think will make a difference, only to abandon them a year later because of a lack of results, commitment, or follow-through. It is also not uncommon to see principals and teachers frustrated and burned out from working long hours on a myriad of initiatives that do not result in higher achievement for their students.

Individual schools and entire school districts must move away from the quick fix and take a systemic approach to school improvement if they want real, sustainable improvement for all students. Long-term improvement can only happen when all pieces of the process for school improvement are in place. This book is about putting those pieces together and implementing a blueprint for school improvement. This book also focuses on how administrators, both at the school and central office level, can approach their work, change what they do, and create a commitment to real lifestyle changes.

## Fundamental Precepts

Just as architects and builders work from a fundamental set of architectural principles and experiences, we use our own set of bedrock beliefs and values that guide our work and shape ideas about how schools can improve. Successful dieters and successful builders use the same basic principles for success—repeated application that results in lasting changes and sustained development. Below are the fundamental beliefs and values that underlie the blueprint for school improvement.

## Schooling Is About Student Learning

For educators, the primary mission of schooling must be focused on student learning. As simple as this sounds, a myriad of other distracters prevail to interrupt this basic mission. Schooling that is focused on learning and academic achievement should be at the top of the list of priorities for educators. Therefore, administrators and teachers must hold true to this mission and put teaching and learning decisions first. This means giving the highest priority to the activities that support top-quality teaching and learning. Only student safety supersedes this mandate.

## Five Core Processes Are Aligned to Improve Schools

The five processes that we use for school improvement are not new to teachers and administrators who diligently seek to raise the bar for their schools. We call these five essentials the blueprint processes.

1. Establishing a mission, vision, and values that guide the general direction of the school and its future actions,
2. Using data analysis, which includes both collecting and interpreting data, for better decision making,
3. Using school improvement planning to guide goals, strategies, decisions, and action steps and to create a working plan for the school,
4. Reshaping professional development to become the engine of school improvement, and
5. Differentiating supervision of teaching and learning to monitor how processes are working inside classrooms.

## Each Process Has Its Own Power Tools to Make the Work Happen

Having a process without practical tools for implementation is like a builder having a blueprint without the materials or tools to construct a home. Successful processes for school improvement come with the kind of power tools that get the job done more efficiently and effectively. Administrators who use these tools frequently and effectively will see sustained results. A description of these tools will be discussed in later chapters.

## The Blueprint Processes Must Be Aligned for School Improvement to Happen

We firmly believe that when school improvement processes are aligned, consistent, strong gains will occur. Many, if not most, schools and districts claim to have all the school improvement processes that are outlined above in place. For example, they have a mission statement, and they analyze data. They have a school improvement plan and regularly conduct professional development activities. They even have supervision strategies in place. What they don't have is alignment. When the processes aren't working in harmony with each other to produce the desired results, time and energy spent ensuring that each process functions alone exceeds the time that is spent when the processes work together. When the blueprint processes are aligned, success in one area reaps results for all the other processes. In her book *Getting Excited About Data* (2004), Edie Holcomb notes, "I have rarely seen a fully aligned system. But I have observed that the districts with the most tightly aligned and data-driven approaches to change and improvement are also those [that are] making a difference in student achievement" (p. 2). Aligning the blueprint processes results in *sustained* improvement.

## School Improvement Is Not Done Until Full Implementation Is Achieved

The work is not completed until every child benefits from the innovations put into place to improve the classroom. In her early days as a school principal, Nancy worked with her faculty to implement several literacy practices. During her daily visits to classrooms, she observed the blueprint practices being applied in a number of classrooms and was overjoyed that the students appeared to be benefiting from the innovations. She even paused to marvel at the power of instructional leadership and its influence on the students in the classroom. Thinking that all was going well, Nancy was very disappointed when the state test results arrived and the improvements were not as she expected. Only a few students benefited from the few teachers who completely embraced the initiatives that were put in place through professional development. After deep reflection and study, she realized that her joy about implementing the program was reserved for only a few teachers who actually followed through on the innovations. Those stark realities led Nancy to begin fully implementing the program for improvement throughout the school.

Every child deserves to have the best practices in the classroom, not just those students who are fortunate enough to have a strong teacher that year. Full implementation means that everyone engages in the school and district improvement efforts at a high level.

## Strong Principals as Instructional Leaders Make Strong Schools with High Achievement

When strong principals become instructional leaders for their staff, they create strong schools with high achievement. The principal must be smart about teaching and learning. There is no shortcut for this practice and no substitute for the critical role of instructional leadership. Therefore, investing in ongoing professional development for principals and setting high expectations for their role as leaders will give them the best chance of fully implementing the blueprint processes in their schools. Through our collective experiences of working with principals, we have seen how aligning the blueprint processes affects the changes that are needed in schools today.

## The Central Office Serves the Schools and Provides the District with a Vision

Central office administrators also serve as leaders for schools by meeting the needs of the school and providing a unifying vision for the district as a whole. The role of the central office is about providing service, not being served. It is about developing and casting a vision for what the district can become and then making that vision possible. Serving schools means caring for their physical needs, such as providing materials, supplies, and facilities and meeting their personnel needs. It also means ensuring that curriculum is aligned to standards and that schools have support for assessment. We believe that central office supervisors, especially those who supervise principals, must be models of instructional leadership. These leaders should serve principals as coaches, mentors, and supervisors.

## Creating Urgency to Improve Performance

Creating a sense of urgency in schools means developing a clear mandate for improvement, one so clear it cannot be ignored. Operating with a sense of urgency includes developing an intense focus, raising levels of concern, and creating a climate where continuous improvement guides all decision making. Schools and districts with a sense of urgency never quit. Their search for improvement moves to the next level because they want all students to learn. A sense of urgency is not reserved for districts that are in dire need of improvement, have limited resources, or are in danger of losing all credibility. Urgency matters to every district and school that clings to the vision of having every student be successful. Until that goal is accomplished, a state of urgency should permeate the work.

## Building Trusting and Respectful Relationships

The ability to form trusting and respectful connections with others greatly influences the chance for success in all other aspects of improving schools. The best practices, programs, and processes rely on people to implement them. The culture of the school and district emanates from the relationships among its members, and without genuine respectful relationships, the chances for instituting the processes for school improvement greatly diminish. One must establish and nurture a sense of trust and respect among those who do the work and those who benefit from it. In discussing the human side of making change in schools, Robert Evans (1996) emphasizes the importance of helping people who implement changes to let go of old ways and welcome new commitments. Building collegial relationships helps to foster collaborative thought and collaborative action.

## Developing an Intense Focus

Developing an intense focus means that school leaders have a laser like commitment to a task. They have clearly defined the pathways for school improvement, they set priorities for progress, and they work without ceasing to see their plans enacted. When schools and districts have an intense focus, nothing deters them from accomplishing their short-term or long-term goals. All of their resources are pointed in one direction, and when the goal is accomplished, their focus moves up to the next level, and they are ready to meet the next challenge. We believe that developing an intense focus helps to set apart leaders who make it to the finish line and are successful with implementing important initiatives and improving their schools. On a practical level, leaders with an intense focus make genuine plans and follow through until they reach their goal, actively seek data to support their progress toward their goals and strategies, and spend significant time in the classrooms to monitor students' learning.

There is a scene in *The Empire Strikes Back* where Luke Skywalker attempts to extract his plane from under swampy waters. He uses the Force, as taught to him by Jedi master Yoda, but he fails to lift the plane because he allows himself to be distracted by noises around him. He believes that the task is impossible. Yoda demonstrates the power of intense focus, and he summons his mastery of the Force to lift the plane from the swamp. Luke expresses his disbelief at what the teacher has done, to which Yoda replies, "That is why you fail." A leader's ability to develop an intense focus will determine his or her overall success towards improving schools.

These precepts guide our thinking and our actions for school improvement. Our ideas did not happen over the course of a few days or even months. These precepts evolved from our experience of working with the processes, making mistakes, and achieving success along the way. These experiences helped us to form the beliefs and values that we express in these precepts.

Throughout this book you will notice that we liken the work of a principal or central office administrator to an architect or builder. Our purpose in using this analogy is twofold. First, we feel this analogy will help readers develop a deeper understanding of the concepts and processes presented throughout the book. Second, it helps to illustrate the necessity for using a common set of tools to keep the work of school improvement on target. It has been our experience that without the tools in this book, we would have had limited success in increasing student achievement. We know that architects or builders would not approach their work without the right tools, and our hope is that, after reading this book, you will do the same.

## Book Overview

We use the following format in each chapter to guide readers throughout the book:

- **Opening Anecdote:** We open each chapter with a brief vignette that is taken directly from our experiences. These anecdotes serve as a bridge to understand why and how the processes in each chapter were developed.
- **Essential Questions:** The essential questions will frame the chapter and serve as the focus for the subsequent discussion.
- **Practical Solutions:** This section contains the meat of each chapter. The practical solutions provide an explanation for the specific tools that we use to facilitate the work.
- **The Role of the Central Office:** Each chapter contains pertinent information for central office administrators. This section addresses the unique needs and demands of this role as it relates to school improvement.
- **Reflections from the Field:** This section provides a closing reflection from our experiences that helps put the preceding discussion into context and deepens readers' understanding. Each reflection is drawn from actual memos that we have used during our tenure as central office leaders. Readers can use these reflections as a model for how central office leaders and principals can develop relationships.
- **Touchstone Texts:** We include a list of references that we use as the foundation for the discussions in the chapters.

# Chapter Overview

## Chapter 1: Developing Curriculum Leadership and Design

**Power Tools: Curriculum Guides and Pacing Curriculum Guide**

The power tools are useless without an energy source. A strong curriculum is the power source for improving schools. Without a rigorous and thoughtful curriculum, the work in classrooms falls short of excellence. Chapter 1 provides fundamental processes for developing and implementing a strong curriculum throughout the district. This chapter also shows readers how to align teaching and learning practices with school improvement efforts. Practical techniques and forms are also included in this chapter to help school leaders create solid curriculum documents in a timely fashion.

## Chapter 2: Aligning the Design for School Improvement

Chapter 2 provides an overview of the five core processes that are necessary for school improvement. This chapter describes how the processes are aligned with each other. Recognizing alignment and its significance and the first blueprint process, developing a mission and vision, are also discussed in this chapter.

## Chapter 3: Making Sense of the Data

**Power Tools: The Black Folder, The State of the Schools Report, and The School Portfolio**

Chapter 3 explains how school leaders can organize data in a way that helps to facilitate their understanding. This chapter also provides an in-depth discussion on developing the State of the Schools report and the school portfolio. The State of the Schools report is a cumulative report that helps administrators understand the big picture and focus on the next direction for the district. The school portfolio is a cumulative report for schools that uses district and school data.

## Chapter 4: Providing Accountability for the Data

**Power Tool: The Data Consultation**

A plethora of data exists in schools today. Chapter 4 shows school leaders what data to use and how to be truly accountable for the information. This chapter also outlines another tool critical in the school improvement process, the data consultation. The data consultation consists of a scheduled conversation between the school administrative team, usually the principal and the assistant principals, and one or more central office administrators. The school portfolio or data collection system, the school improvement plan, and the school professional development plan serve as the primary resources for the discussion.

## Chapter 5: Working the Plan for School Improvement

**Power Tool: The School Improvement Plan**

Chapter 5 focuses on developing a school improvement plan that actually drives improvement. This chapter emphasizes how the school improvement plan can be aligned with the other blueprint processes, and it also shows the important distinctions among goals, strategies, and action steps. Techniques for engaging and monitoring the staff in the school improvement process are also included in this chapter.

## Chapter 6: Developing Powerful Professional Development

**Power Tools: The Professional Development Plan and Look Fors**

Long before No Child Left Behind, educators understood the importance of highly qualified staff. The conundrum was how to align professional development efforts with school improvement processes and hold people accountable for implementation. Chapter 6 focuses on developing a meaningful and relevant professional development plan that aligns with the other blueprint processes and raises student achievement. Look fors, another power tool that helps school leaders align and fully implement school improvement processes, are also discussed in this chapter.

## Chapter 7: Supervising Teaching, Learning, and People

**Power Tools: Walkthroughs and The Postobservation Conference**

Just as architects have tools for monitoring the progress of new construction, school and district leaders must also have tools for monitoring people and progress. Too many schools have engaged in school reform efforts without planning time for actually doing and maintaining the work. Chapter 7 addresses how supervising teaching, learning, and people fits in a framework for school improvement. The walkthrough and the postobservation conference are two power tools for this framework. The walkthrough is a tool for monitoring the school improvement plan and professional development efforts. Examples and benefits of different types of walkthroughs are discussed in this chapter. The postobservation conference is also examined as a part of differentiated supervision.

### Chapter 8: Creating Leaders for School Improvement

**Power Tools: The Weekly Message, Principals' Academy, and Monthly Principal PD Meeting**

If the right tools are placed in the wrong hands, a successful structure cannot be guaranteed. The role that school and central office leaders play will determine whether the structure will have an effect on student achievement. Chapter 8 goes beyond identifying the essential qualities of a strong instructional leader and provides concepts and tools that help all leaders keep their focus on teaching and learning. This chapter also discusses professional development for principals and building and developing relationships with mutual trust and respect among all school leaders.

## Processes and Power Tools

Increasing student achievement is no small task. An architect plans and designs a project using broad architectural concepts and processes. A builder and his crew use power tools to make the work a reality. The concepts (i.e., major ideas), processes (i.e., how to approach the work), and tools (i.e., devices used to do the work) are necessary for solid construction. When we approach improving schools, we have to be both the architect and the builder. We need to know the broad concepts of school improvement, the processes and action steps that are needed to achieve a particular goal, and the specific tools to help make the work happen. A list of the broad concepts, school improvement processes, and accompanying tools is found in Figure I.1. The most successful schools and districts understand that these concepts, processes, and tools are necessary for improving schools and aligning the blueprint processes. Chapter 2 will discuss alignment in more detail.

FIGURE I.1 **Processes, Concepts, and Power Tools**

| Processes | Concepts | Power Tools |
|---|---|---|
| Mission, Vision, Values | | |
| Data Analysis | | The Black Folder<br>The State of the Schools Report<br>The School Portfolio<br>Data Consultation |
| School Improvement Planning | | School Improvement Plan |
| Professional Development | | Professional Development Plan<br>Look Fors |
| Supervising Teaching, Learning, and People | | Walkthroughs<br>Postobservation Conference |
| | Curriculum | Curriculum Guides<br>Pacing Curriculum Guide |
| | Leadership | The Weekly Message<br>Principals' Academy<br>Monthly Principal PD Meeting |

# 1

# Developing Curriculum Leadership and Design

Do what you always do, get what you always get.

—*Source unknown*

Ann had just completed a long, arduous revision process for a science curriculum, and she was feeling the satisfaction of a job well done. She had worked with a diligent, broad-based committee of educators for three years. Their hard work was evident by the shiny, new curriculum guides that were placed gingerly on the shelves of classrooms across the district. As Ann walked through classrooms and talked with principals and teachers regarding the new curriculum, she observed, much to her surprise, that little had changed in regard to science instruction, especially in scientific inquiry. Teachers were teaching many isolated activities, but they were not engaged in the process. Ann had spent hours with the team reviewing state and national standards and discussing their implications. The team engaged in an in-depth analysis of the district data and identified the strengths and weaknesses of the current curriculum. Surveys were distributed to parents, teachers, staff, and students requesting their feedback on the science curriculum. So, why had nothing changed?

The status quo was maintained in this district because the curriculum team didn't have any discussions on the best instructional practices. Ann had assumed that the team members already had a solid foundation on these practices, so they jumped right into writing the curriculum. In her haste to get the guides produced, she made a critical error. By not reading, reflecting on, and discussing the best instructional practices, the curriculum team was not equipped to develop a curriculum that would result in long-lasting changes in instruction and student achievement.

## Essential Question

- How do you align curriculum and instruction through the curriculum development process?

When we hear the phrase "the good old days," it is usually uttered with a sense of longing and a fondness for a return to the way things used to be. When it comes to curriculum development, this sentiment would not hold true for many teachers and administrators who have been involved in writing curriculum over the last 10 years. In the old days, curriculum development started with a basic question: "What do we want our students to know?" Fortunately, the question of what to teach has been addressed through state and national standards. But now that state and national standards are tied to accountability measures, the questions needed to develop curriculum have changed. Federal and state leaders have spent large amounts of time and energy painstakingly identifying what and when students should learn something. Now that they have taken care of these concerns, we can shift our focus. Rather than lament what might feel like a loss of autonomy or local control, we feel that this guidance from the federal and state level can help curriculum departments move into an important new era. This new era will allow us to spend more time focusing on aligning curriculum and instruction, rather than developing curriculum guides. We have shifted from focusing on *what* to focusing on *how*.

## Aligning Curriculum and Instruction

A few years ago there was a story about several new homes that were literally sliding down the slope where they had been built. These homes were well-designed, luxurious, and located in an exclusive subdivision; however, they were built on land that was slowly eroding. Because these homes were not built on a solid foundation, their design and craftsmanship were rendered useless; the houses could not be occupied. Building a home that will stand the test of time requires both a solid foundation and a sound design plan. It is not an either/or proposition. The same holds true for curriculum and instruction.

Too many times we have entered classrooms and observed teachers using research-based strategies on insignificant content. An effective instructional practice loses effectiveness if the curriculum isn't strong enough. For example, using the Four Square Writing Method (Gould & Gould, 1999) will not help improve students' writing if we ask students to write on contrived, inane topics such as how it feels to be a puddle in springtime. Even though the Four Square method is an effective strategy, this process is lost on students if they aren't asked to write as a response to reading and thinking.

Conversely, having high academic standards isn't enough if they are not implemented through powerful instructional methods. Unfortunately, many of us have spent time writing guides that outlined great standards only to have them sit on the shelf while classroom instruction remains unchanged. Curriculum and instruction are interdependent, and curriculum work needs to be approached with this important precept in mind.

We use two sets of research findings as the foundation for developing curriculum. First, a common curriculum with clear, intelligible standards that are aligned with appropriate assessments is critical to school improvement (Fullan & Stiegelbauer, 1991; Marzano, 2003; Rosenholtz, 1991). The lack of a clearly articulated curriculum hinders improvement efforts and, according to Mike Schmoker (2006), results in curriculum chaos. Second, in order for schools to improve, school personnel need to function as professional learning communities (DuFour & Eaker, 1998; Wagner, 2004; Wise, 2004). Teachers need ongoing opportunities to meet and plan common units and assessments. It is extremely difficult to develop professional learning communities if teachers are teaching different concepts at different points during the year. In order for districtwide improvement to happen, teachers must have the time to revise and develop curriculum that is focused on instruction.

Leaders can help teachers improve student achievement by implementing best instructional practices for teaching high content standards. In other words, school leaders must pay attention to both the curriculum ("what") and the instruction ("how"). The following fundamental concepts will ensure that the curriculum is aligned with instruction and will lay the cornerstone for curriculum development work:

- **Learn, Then Do.** Powerful professional development needs to be embedded in the curriculum development process.
- **Develop Leadership Structure.** Structures need to be in place to allow curriculum developers and leaders to supervise or work closely with building principals.

## Learn, Then Do

Ann's experience illustrates what happens when the desire to produce a product trumps the process. When she ignored the curriculum development team's need to study effective instructional practices in science education, the overall quality of the final product was compromised. Writing curriculum isn't just about producing a guide. It includes defining what students need to know and do and giving teachers proven practices that will work with their specific content area. In order to avoid the pitfall of creating curriculum without a focus on instruction, we recommend two phases to manage the work. The first phase, planning and development, is used when an in-depth curriculum revision is needed; the second phase, review and evaluation, can help a team manage the curriculum after it is developed and ensure that it is implemented effectively.

Curriculum study and writing is a continuous improvement process, and subject-area curriculum teams will drive curriculum development for a district. Depending on the size of the district, representatives from every building, grade, and subject area should make up the teams. If the district is large, divide the teams by elementary and secondary schools. If the team is divided by elementary and secondary schools, it is critical for team members from transition grade levels (e.g., 5th and 8th grade teachers and administrators) to have opportunities to discuss grade-level matriculation. Representatives from other departments, such as library media, gifted and talented education, special education, ESL, Title I, and administrators from each elementary, middle, and high school should also be included on the team.

Simply having representative administrators from the central office on the curriculum team is not enough. The central office curriculum leader needs to ensure that building principals who are engaged in the curriculum and instruction process go beyond participating in meetings and help them make high levels of engagement with teaching and learning happen in their schools. The leadership structure section at the end of this chapter will address this concept in-depth.

The curriculum development team should review each curriculum document on an annual basis and have an in-depth revision and update for the curriculum on a six-to-eight year cycle as determined by the curriculum revision cycle. This development cycle is a critical piece to managing the work and the curriculum budget.

Figure 1.1 outlines each step during the planning and development phase. Each step includes specific promising practices to follow ("do's") and pitfalls to avoid ("don'ts").

FIGURE 1.1 **The Planning and Development Process**

| Step | Curriculum Goal | Instructional Goal | Time-frame | End Product |
|---|---|---|---|---|
| **Step 1:** Establish the Foundation | • Analyze state and national standards | • Identify and begin reading book for study group | Year 1 | • Philosophy and rationale for curriculum |
| **Step 2:** Data Analysis | • Review national, state, and local test data<br>• Review surveys from parents, teachers, students, and administrators | • Debrief book chapters<br>• Identify effective instructional practices for the content area through book study sessions and related articles | Year 1 | • Goals for graduates<br>• Course descriptions<br>• Effective instructional practices |
| **Step 3:** Assessments | • Develop benchmark assessments around big ideas in the curriculum | • Learn how to write constructed-response and performance event questions<br>• Develop rubrics | Summer Curriculum Camp | • District performance assessments<br>• Rubrics |
| **Step 4:** Writing | • Develop scope and sequence and curriculum map | | Summer Curriculum Camp | • Scope and sequence<br>• Curriculum map |
| **Step 5:** Resources Review | • Review relevant texts with the team | • Develop textbook review form<br>• Identify best instructional practices | Summer Curriculum Camp | • Texts selected for pilot (2–3 per grade span) |
| **Step 6:** Pilot Process | • Teachers pilot two units from each pilot text | • Develop instructional policy for curriculum | Year 2 | • Select resources for curriculum |
| **Step 7:** Board Approval | • Board of education reviews curriculum | • Board of education reviews instruction policy | Year 2 | • Board of education approves curriculum and instruction |
| **Step 8:** Staff Development | • Staff trains with new curriculum and materials | • Train curriculum team members as trainers and curriculum mentors | Year 3 | • Post curriculum on the Web<br>• Select district trainers |

| FIGURE 1.1 | The Planning and Development Process *(continued)* | | | |
|---|---|---|---|---|
| **Step 9:** Implementation | • Principals monitor implementation through curriculum maps | • Mentors help monitor implementation in buildings | Years 3-7 | • Increased student achievement |

## Step 1: Establish the Foundation

This step sets the tone for the entire planning and development process.

### DO

Do make sure that you spend significant time with the team to help them understand state and national standards. Most state assessments are based on national standards; therefore it is imperative that teachers have explicit knowledge about what students are expected to know. These standards are the driving force for curriculum development and will help teachers move away from negative thinking, such as "We've always done it this way" or "Our students won't be able to handle the information at that grade."

### DON'T

Don't forget to identify a book or a series of articles that will serve as the touchstone text for the curriculum revision process. Studying a book or a set of articles will serve as the cornerstone for the professional discussions that the team will have over the next few years. Thus, it is imperative to select texts that have proven instructional strategies instead of choosing lesson activities. The key in selecting materials for a group study is to understand the current district achievement data and the gaps that exist in teaching and learning practices throughout the district. For example, during a language arts curriculum revision, a preK–12 team chose *Mosaic of Thought* (Keene & Zimmerman, 1997) as their touchstone text and read selected chapters from *Strategies That Work* (Harvey & Goudvis, 2007) and *Reading with Meaning* (Miller, 2002). These selections helped them focus on their district's low reading comprehension scores on state and national tests and begin implementing reading strategies across the content areas. They also helped the team understand and identify what comprehension strategy instruction should look like in the classroom. Once the team had this understanding, developing a curriculum based on strategies that proficient readers could use was much easier.

## Step 2: Data Analysis

This step focuses on developing a common understanding of the district's needs. The goal is for all team members to identify strengths and weaknesses in the district's curriculum by analyzing student achievement data.

### DO

Do help teachers understand the implications of test scores beyond the scope of their own classroom. Make sure that teachers work in vertical teams to discuss achievement gaps at all levels. While more teachers have an opportunity to collaborate with their grade-level peers, it is extremely rare for teachers to discuss teaching and learning with their colleagues outside of their consecutive grade levels. When teachers have opportunities to talk with other teachers across all grade levels, the team broadens their understanding of major curriculum issues and begins to move from functioning as a group of individuals to working as a professional learning community.

According to DuFour (2004), a professional learning community is a team of teachers who meet on a regular basis to establish curriculum standards and collaborate on how to teach these standards. This is exactly the role that the district curriculum team should play. According to Marzano (2003), one of the most important factors that influence student achievement is developing a guaranteed and viable curriculum. This type of curriculum helps teachers identify a set of relevant standards and ensures that these standards are taught. In order to develop a guaranteed and viable curriculum, the curriculum development team must operate as a professional learning community.

There are two reasons for establishing a professional learning community at the district level. First, there is a general consensus among educational researchers that professional learning communities are one of the most promising strategies for significant and sustained school improvement. Members of the research community have developed a collective statement that supports the use of professional learning communities (Schmoker, 2006). The tools and processes outlined in this book are designed so that sustained improvements in achievement happen not only at the building level, but also at the district level. If long-term, sustained student achievement is the goal, district-level professional learning communities are not optional. Second, a district-level professional learning community can establish a model for developing curriculum for building principals and help them understand how to establish curriculum development teams in their schools.

## DON'T

Don't assume that all the members on the curriculum development team know enough about the topic to complete all the tasks at a high level. It is impossible to form a team where every member comes to the table with sufficient curricular and instructional knowledge. Some team members may need more experience or more opportunities to reflect on the topic from a different perspective. Savvy and successful curriculum leaders recognize that serving on a writing team is a high-level professional development task. These leaders know how to carry out the critical role of developing and training members of the writing team. Thus, professional development for the writing team must be embedded with information regarding what the data mean, strategies for including the most effective instructional practices in the content area, and data about the gaps in the current curriculum.

While it is necessary to produce a written curriculum to meet state and district requirements, the document becomes a by-product of learning how to deeply connect powerful curriculum with proven instructional methods.

## Step 3: Assessments

The purpose of this step is to help the curriculum development team establish local benchmarks that will help teachers identify how well students understand the big ideas outlined in the curriculum standards. Starting curriculum development with assessments is not a new idea. Wiggins and McTighe's (1998) backward design model, which begins with identifying desired results, is a widely adopted standard for curriculum development. The objective of the backward design model is to help curriculum developers create units of study around major concepts in the curriculum. Units are designed to help students develop deep understandings of the concepts that are taught. Wiggins and McTighe recognize that teaching that is consistently geared toward deep and sophisticated understanding at all times is both impossible and impractical. They acknowledge that students also need to acquire basic skills such as learning math facts and reciting the alphabet. Wiggins and McTighe's work is significant because it is focused on understanding rather than simply covering curriculum.

Creating common assessments at the district level will help the team develop an understanding of what is really important for students to know. The central office administrator can use common assessments to establish benchmarks for the district and to monitor improvements and efficiency of district curriculum; however, we do not advocate developing units at the district level. Units need to be created at the building level through school-based professional learning communities.

## DO

Do develop standards and criteria for creating quality assessments before writing. Make sure that you are spending a considerable amount of time on this step because this is where the majority of the writing work will be required from team members. These assessments will drive your curriculum development and resource selection. Team members need to understand how to write effective assessments and discuss the process for collecting these assessment data so that they can be relevant to classroom and district practice. Professional development on assessing literacy is also critical to this step. The team needs to know how to write assessments that align to the standards and big ideas in the curriculum. Do not feel as though the team needs to reinvent the wheel when writing assessments. There are many sources that the team can use to get started. Consider the following:

- Examine tests from texts or other supplementary materials that the district has already purchased. Some of these materials may work well and may only need minor adjustments to meet your district's standards.
- Evaluate state assessments samples. Model local benchmark assessments on state tests when appropriate.
- Share assessments with other districts. Improving teaching and learning for all students is the mission of public education. Do not let competitiveness or turf issues stand in the way of creating real change for students.

## DON'T

Don't try to develop assessments after school or during a monthly professional development day. Make time to commit to this work when you have the team together for an extended period. The costs for setting aside this time for both small and large districts can interfere with this recommendation; however, if the mission of school is learning, then writing curriculum for teaching and learning and ensuring its implementation warrants top priority in budget allocation. To do otherwise slights the integrity of instructional leadership.

Ann used Curriculum Camp to accomplish this work with her team. Curriculum Camp is five intense days of curriculum work during which the curriculum development team can work without interruptions. Ann and her team usually conduct their Curriculum Camp during the week before summer school begins. The team spends most of their time at the Curriculum Camp writing assessments. This process can take two to four days, depending on the subject area. Figure 1.2 provides an overview of the schedule for Curriculum Camp. Steps 3 through 5 are accomplished during the camp. Steps 1 and 2 are accomplished during the school year prior to the summer Curriculum Camp.

FIGURE 1.2

**Curriculum Camp Schedule**

| | Content | Step in Development Cycle* |
|---|---|---|
| Monday | Training on developing quality assessments (whole group)<br>• Learn how to write constructed response items<br>• Develop rubrics | Step 3 |
| Tuesday | Develop assessments (grade-level teams)<br>• Monitor for quality control | Step 4 |
| Wednesday | Finish assessments (grade-level teams)<br>• Monitor for quality control | Step 4 |
| Thursday | Develop curriculum review form (whole group)<br>• Begin material review | Step 5 |
| Friday | Select materials for review<br>• Grade-level teams identify units for pilot | Step 5 |

*Steps 1 and 2 occur during the school year in scheduled meetings.

In small districts or districts with limited resources, conducting a Curriculum Camp may be difficult. These districts need to reexamine how they are spending their current budget and reallocate or reorganize their funding in order to provide large blocks of time for their staff to work. Failure to organize this time wisely will result in a fragmented curriculum and frustrated teachers who spend the majority of their time trying to figure out what they did at the last meeting, instead of having rich discussions about teaching and learning. Providing a significant block of time for the curriculum development team to do this work promotes depth in the curriculum, allows time for reflection, and communicates the importance of this process.

## Step 4: Writing

This step will help the team begin to create supporting curriculum documents that teachers can use to implement the curriculum in the classroom. Developing a curriculum guide is an important step in this process. A template for a sample curriculum guide can be found in Figure 1.3.

### Power Tool: Curriculum Guides and Pacing Curriculum Guide

One of the most important power tools for writing and implementing content is a curriculum map. The curriculum map is the big picture that provides a clear guide for important concepts and assessments that need to be taught throughout the year. The benefits of a fully implemented curriculum map include the following:

- Ensuring that every child in the district receives the same content
- Helping teachers see curriculum connections between content areas
- Promoting integration with teachers and specialists outside of the core content areas, such special education teachers and library media specialists; this will help these professionals align relevant concepts in their curriculum with classroom curriculum topics that occur during the year
- Providing administrators with a vehicle to manage all of the curricular areas
- Ensuring that the teacher's favorite topic or unit is taught only when core curricular concepts have been mastered or not at all if it does not have relevance

Curriculum maps, like curriculum guides, will raise student achievement only when they are fully implemented by every teacher for every child. Creating maps and guides without full implementation is like owning a power tool without having electricity or batteries. The central office administrator and the building administrator are both responsible for monitoring implementation. For extensive information on curriculum mapping, see Jacobs (2004). An example of a curriculum map that we use can be found in Figure 1.4.

## FIGURE 1.3 Curriculum Guide Template

**Grade Level:** Kindergarten
**Course:** Mathematics
**Master Objective:** Understand numbers, ways of representing numbers, relationships among numbers, and number systems.

| Facilitating Objective/ Activities: | Strategy | Bloom's Taxonomy | Cross-Curricular Tie |
|---|---|---|---|
| A. Rote count to 100 | Read, write, and compare numbers | Analysis | |
| B. Connect number words (orally) and the quantities they represent | Compose and decompose numbers | Application | |

**Assessment:**

| **Strands:** | Numbers and Operations |
|---|---|
| **State Standards: Performance:** | MA 1, 6 |
| **State Standards: Knowledge:** | 1.6, 1.10 |

FIGURE 1.4
**Curriculum Map Example**

| 1st Quarter | | 2nd Quarter | | 3rd Quarter | | 4th Quarter | |
|---|---|---|---|---|---|---|---|
| **Differentiated Reading Instruction** | **Comprehension Strategy Instruction** | **Differentiated Reading Instruction** | **Comprehension Strategy Instruction** | **Differentiated Reading Instruction** | **Comprehension Strategy Instruction** | **Differentiated Reading Instruction** | **Comprehension Strategy Instruction** |
| Resources:<br>■ Rigby Literacy Guided reading books<br>■ Reading resource library<br>■ Literacy placemat<br><br>Objectives:<br>R1C, R1D, R1F, R1G, R1H, R1I, R1J, R2D | Resources:<br>■ CQ—Vol. 1<br><br>Strategies:<br>■ Using and extending what you know<br>■ Creating and using images<br>■ Monitoring meaning<br>■ Asking questions<br><br>Objectives:<br>R1G, R1I, R1J, R1D, R1E, R3A, L1A | Resources:<br>■ Rigby Literacy Guided reading books<br>■ Reading resource library<br>■ Literacy placemat<br><br>Objectives:<br>R1C, R1D, R1F, R1G, R1H, R1I, R1J, R2D | Resources:<br>■ CQ—Vol. 2<br><br>Strategies:<br>■ Asking questions<br>■ Determining important ideas and themes<br><br>Objectives:<br>R1D, R1E, R1J, R2D, R3C, L1A | Resources:<br>■ Rigby Literacy Guided reading books<br>■ Reading resource library<br>■ Literacy placemat<br><br>Objectives:<br>R1C, R1D, R1F, R1G, R1H, R1I, R1J, R2D | Resources:<br>■ CQ—Vol. 3<br><br>Strategies:<br>■ Synthesizing<br>■ Inferring<br>■ Monitoring meaning<br><br>Objectives:<br>R1D, R1G, R1H, R1J, R2C, R3A, R3C, L1A | Resources:<br>■ Rigby Literacy Guided reading books<br>■ Reading resource library<br>■ Literacy placemat<br><br>Objectives:<br>R1C, R1D, R1F, R1G, R1H, R1I, R1J, R2D | Resources:<br>■ CQ—Vol. 4<br><br>Strategies:<br>■ Inferring<br>■ Synthesizing<br>■ Using and extending knowledge<br><br>Objectives:<br>R1D, R1E, R1G, R1H, R1I, R1J, R2C, R3A, R3C, L1A |

### DO

Do develop a check-and-balance procedure for reviewing the work of the curriculum development team. Devise a system that ensures that anything produced, such as the scope and sequence or a curriculum map, is viewed by both vertical and grade-level teams. This may seem like common sense, but the sheer volume of work that is produced during a curriculum revision is daunting, and it takes a systematic approach to maintain coherence and quality.

### DON'T

Don't write activities or lessons. At the district level, these documents should serve as a guide only. Spending time writing lessons and activities is ineffective for several reasons. First, you are assuming that you know the students in the classroom. It is frivolous to write a lesson in the absence of knowing about the students who will receive the lesson. Second, it is the teacher's role as the professional educator to develop lessons that will meet students' needs. Teachers should have the autonomy to develop lessons around the district's standards and curriculum. As teachers do more work in professional learning communities, they will learn how to develop common lessons and assessments at the classroom level.

## Step 5: Resource Review

During this phase of curriculum development, the team reviews and selects resources that align with the standards, grade-level expectations, and assessments that the team developed. The team will typically review five or more different resources and narrow them down to two. These materials will become the resources that are piloted in the next phase.

### DO

Do develop a materials review form prior to looking at any products. It is easy to fall into the trap of rushing to review glitzy packages. Looking at materials before establishing criteria causes two major problems. First, it allows the publisher to dictate curriculum, and second, it perpetuates the notion that the texts are the curriculum instead of a resource. Curriculum leaders are responsible for shifting teachers' perceptions from teaching a book to teaching students. They are also responsible for providing professional development to teachers during this process.

One way to avoid having materials taking precedence over curriculum is to take at least half a day to develop a form that synthesizes what the team has learned through the book study conducted throughout the year. This form will help the team look at all the materials with similar eyes. The team can also use the form to identify what is important for a specific subject area from both a content and pedagogical standpoint. This is also an ideal time to identify strong, effective instructional practices that will help the team search for materials that most easily lend themselves to their current teaching methods. Finally, it is also important during this step to analyze information from parents, students, and staff surveys when developing the curriculum review form. Figure 1.5 provides an example of a textbook review form.

### DON'T

Don't rush into bringing publishers in to speak to the team. Instead of having companies come in and do a sales pitch, districts have several options. One option is to use curriculum money to send representatives from the curriculum development team to state and national conferences for specific curricular areas. Not only will the team learn more about effective instructional practices by attending the conference, they can spend time in the exhibit hall identifying possible resources that also deserve consideration for a pilot. Samples can be requested, reviewed, and narrowed down back at the district.

If traveling to conferences is too costly, the team can request samples from publishers and set up an exhibit at the district level. Team members can browse through materials at designated times during the school year. Avoid the temptation to accept special meetings, lunches, or gifts from the companies that are aimed at influencing your selection.

## Step 6: Pilot Process

During this phase of development, the team pilots all sets of materials with students.

### DO

Do pilot all materials with students for an extended period of time. Make sure that the teachers who are participating in the pilot use all materials with their

FIGURE 1.5

## Textbook Review Form

**Textbook Evaluation Scoring Guide**

**Text:**________________________________________

**Publisher:** ________________________________________

Please evaluate the following criteria with 1 as the LOWEST and 5 as the HIGHEST rating.

| **Content** | | | | | |
|---|---|---|---|---|---|
| Aligns with geography strand | 1 | 2 | 3 | 4 | 5 |
| Aligns with history strand | 1 | 2 | 3 | 4 | 5 |
| Aligns with economics strand | 1 | 2 | 3 | 4 | 5 |
| Aligns with civics strand | 1 | 2 | 3 | 4 | 5 |
| Strong assessments that include authentic assessments | 1 | 2 | 3 | 4 | 5 |
| Provides opportunities for differentiated instruction | 1 | 2 | 3 | 4 | 5 |
| Provides opportunities for students to communicate in writing | 1 | 2 | 3 | 4 | 5 |
| Developmentally appropriate map skills | 1 | 2 | 3 | 4 | 5 |
| Cause and effect incorporated for major concepts | 1 | 2 | 3 | 4 | 5 |

| **Pedagogical Approach** | | | | | |
|---|---|---|---|---|---|
| Incorporates technology | 1 | 2 | 3 | 4 | 5 |
| Integrates with other subjects | 1 | 2 | 3 | 4 | 5 |
| Variety of teaching strategies included | 1 | 2 | 3 | 4 | 5 |
| Developmentally appropriate content | 1 | 2 | 3 | 4 | 5 |
| Developmentally appropriate reading level | 1 | 2 | 3 | 4 | 5 |
| Engaging instruction and activities (brain compatible) | 1 | 2 | 3 | 4 | 5 |

| **Organization and Structure of Materials** | | | | | |
|---|---|---|---|---|---|
| Teacher support materials provided | 1 | 2 | 3 | 4 | 5 |
| Age-level appropriate appealing materials | 1 | 2 | 3 | 4 | 5 |
| Home-school connection | 1 | 2 | 3 | 4 | 5 |
| Clearly organized student materials | 1 | 2 | 3 | 4 | 5 |
| Clearly organized guides (teacher-friendly) | 1 | 2 | 3 | 4 | 5 |

Things I really liked about this series:

________________________________________

________________________________________

Concerns I have about this series:

________________________________________

________________________________________

Other comments:

________________________________________

________________________________________

students for at least six to eight weeks. It is not enough to have teachers attend a meeting after school, listen to a sales pitch, receive a few freebies, and flip through the materials. Teachers must have an opportunity to use the materials with students and make sure the materials align with the instructional sequence for an entire unit of study. One resource cannot be expected to meet all the needs of any content area; therefore, teachers should use materials for a longer period of time to help them realize where supplemental materials may be needed.

Depending on the size of the district, at least one teacher from each school may need to participate in the pilot. Although teachers do not teach the same units simultaneously during the pilot, this design gives teachers opportunities to discuss different approaches to using the same content. This process is also efficient for managing the amount of materials needed to run the pilot. Figure 1.6 outlines how to handle this process.

FIGURE 1.6 **Resource Pilot Process**

| Class and Pilot Unit | School A | School B |
| --- | --- | --- |
| | **Grade 3** | **Grade 3** |
| Earth Science – Rocks | October – Text A | October – Text B |
| Life Science – Life cycle | January – Text B | January – Text A |

## DON'T

Don't be afraid to think outside the box when it comes to adopting materials. If the materials in the pilot do not meet the needs of the students in your district, take a step back and think differently about what may be needed. For example, maybe a social studies textbook isn't necessary, but a set of expository books that aligns with the standards might work better. Don't settle for materials that won't help meet both the curriculum standards and the instructional philosophy.

## Step 7: Board Approval

This step involves updating and asking the board of education to adopt the new curriculum.

## DO

Do keep the board of education informed *throughout* the process. Make sure that the teams provide a yearly curriculum update to the board that briefly outlines the major projects and initiatives that will be undertaken during the year and share the processes used to develop curriculum. Skipping this step can put the board in a reactive mode if they are challenged by community members regarding a new initiative. This may also result in the initiative either being rejected or pulled before full implementation is reached.

Ann learned this lesson the hard way when she worked on a mathematics curriculum revision. After reviewing national and state standards and analyzing achievement and course enrollment data, the team decided to use an integrated approach to mathematics at the high school level rather than the traditional Algebra I, Geometry, Algebra II sequence. Even though Ann worked through the process with the team, she knew that there were one or two high school teachers who were anxious about this reform. She also failed to realize the importance of informing the board along the way. When anxious teachers or parents grumbled to board members who had little or no information about the rationale for the change to the curriculum or the process for making this decision, Ann was on the hot seat and had to scramble to provide the board with the pertinent information. Although she weathered this controversy and both the test scores and the number of students enrolled in higher level math classes increased significantly, for the next five years, when she addressed the board, she knew that all the questions directed toward her would be associated with mathematics and how teachers engaged in the curriculum revision process.

## DON'T

Don't make it all about the books. Make sure that the board adopts the curriculum, including the goals, philosophy, standards, and grade-level expectations, before the resources. Resources should be discussed and presented, but they should not be the only focus. Instead, curriculum maps and guides and their content should be highlighted during the presentation. For example, a district that is moving toward balanced literacy should spend time discussing the benefits of this approach and what this type of instruction looks like in classrooms.

## Step 8: Staff Development

This is one of the most critical phases of the process and needs to be ongoing. Without this step, the rest of the revision process is useless.

### DO

Do pay attention to instruction throughout the process. As the team articulates the instructional philosophy, work on bringing the rest of the district on board with where you are headed. This process will look different depending on the content area. Using the previous example of a district moving toward balanced literacy, the first step is to define balanced literacy and to develop guiding principles. Then, while the team is working on developing the curriculum, the curriculum department can work with teachers and schools throughout the district and discuss topics such as what balanced literacy means and what a literacy block looks like. Taking these steps is extremely helpful, especially if the district is making a major shift in instructional practices. If a district waits until the guides are completely developed, then teachers will be focused on the curriculum ("what") and give minimal attention to the instruction ("how").When curriculum development team members don't have enough professional development focused on supporting curriculum, a curriculum development revision simply results in teachers teaching from a new book, instead of applying proven practices.

### DON'T

Don't forget to design professional development that puts the responsibility for implementing the curriculum at the building level. An increasing amount of evidence shows that traditional approaches to professional development are ineffective (Joyce & Showers, 2002). It is crucial to design a more comprehensive system for implementation. This could include adding more building-based coaches and mentors, and it could also mean tailoring implementation based on the size and resources of your district. The point is to *plan* for ongoing professional development that leads to implementation. An expert needs to be identified and trained at each building. This individual will help to ensure that the correct instructional practices and content are being implemented. Ignoring this important concept will result in the new curriculum feeling like the "flavor of the month" rather than a district initiative that will help students learn.

## Step 9: Implementation

This step is where the rubber meets the road. If done right, this part of the work can be the most difficult.

### DO

Do expect instruction to improve and, if it does, collect evidence to monitor the difference. Use the assessments developed by the team to help measure whether the curriculum is meeting the needs of all learners. You should also use national, state, and local assessments to determine the efficacy of the curriculum. The national and state results will help you to look at big-picture trends, while local assessments will help to pinpoint certain areas that may need more attention. When analyzing local data, look for any concepts where there are low scores for a specific group of students. If this occurs, reexamine how those concepts are being taught and addressed in the curriculum.

### DON'T

Don't be afraid to regroup as needed. Curriculum development is like buying a new car. The minute you drive it off the lot, the car is never the same, and after driving the car for awhile, you might find one or two features you would have liked to have had instead. In other words, expect that once teachers and students start using the curriculum on a larger scale, there will be some issues to discuss. Although the curriculum development team may be frustrated because they worked so hard to develop the new curriculum, this is a good problem because it means that teachers are using the curriculum. Curriculum leaders need to help the team understand that revisions are a natural part of the process and plan accordingly. In one district, after rolling out the new science curriculum, teachers complained that they were not sure what the expectations were for scientific inquiry. The team reexamined the curriculum and found that different scientific terms were being used at different grade levels. The team regrouped and identified developmentally appropriate inquiry language and processes to prepare students for the next level of science instruction. These types of issues illustrate why the curriculum development team cannot stop meeting after the curriculum is developed. After completing a major revision, the team can move into the review and evaluation phase.

## Review and Evaluation

One of the reasons why curriculum work is so challenging is that it is never done. Once the team has developed the curriculum, it is imperative that processes are in place to ensure that the teaching and learning in the content area is helping students achieve. One way to make this happen is to have the curriculum teams meet on an ongoing basis. This means that all of the teams, including science, mathematics, reading and language arts, social studies, career and technical education, art, music, physical education and health, and international languages, need to meet at least twice a year. These meetings are important, especially if these teams were not involved in the in-depth revision process outlined in this chapter.

The first meeting should be held early in the year. The goal of this meeting is to review data to determine if minor adjustments to the curriculum need to be made. For example, if the team reviewed assessment data and found that mathematics computation scores were low at the elementary level, then the team would develop a system to ensure that timed tests were given to students in elementary grades. The team may also find that students in social studies classes aren't able to use maps and globes. The team would work on developing support for that aspect of the curriculum. The key is to make decisions based on student achievement data.

Survey data from teachers and parents may also be helpful, but use caution when analyzing these data. If the teachers are in the early stages of implementation and a major change occurs in the curricular area, the survey data may reflect natural frustration associated with the change process. For curriculum leaders, it is important to be cognizant of this frustration. It does not always mean that a change needs to be made. Ann's experience from the beginning of the chapter is a good example of staying the course. If Ann had read the teachers' surveys alone, she would have surely changed directions; however, because she relied heavily on student data, she stayed the course, and it turned out to have the best results for students.

The second meeting needs to occur in the spring. The goal of this meeting is to share progress and updates regarding the initiatives identified in the prior meeting. Typically, the entire curriculum team does not need to work on these adjustments. In a small district, a subcommittee could be pulled together to work on the adjustments, or in a large district, the curriculum department would be responsible for these changes. The key is to make sure that the work gets done and to keep everyone accountable.

## Aligning the Structure with Leadership

Alignment is a central concept in this book. When we say the word alignment, for many people it conjures up the idea of an automobile. If alignment is thought about in those terms, it is easy to understand that full alignment isn't just about the vehicle. Keeping the car aligned has a lot to do with the driver and the team that supports the driver. Watching a NASCAR race makes this point obvious. It isn't the fastest car that wins; it is the fastest car with the most skilled driver who has an expert team backing him up. The same theory holds true for curriculum development. It takes an expert team to develop the curriculum, but it is critically important to put the curriculum in the hands of the principal. Without a principal's leadership and ownership of the curriculum and instruction, teachers and students do not move forward. (For more discussion on alignment, see Chapter 2.)

In far too many districts, curriculum development is treated as an activity separate from schools. Curriculum development is viewed apart from regular school as something done in an esoteric ivory tower at the central office and handed down to teachers and principals. One of the fundamental precepts we mentioned in the Introduction is that the mission of schooling is student learning. Curriculum and instruction are critical to achieving this mission and need to have priority. The principal needs to be informed every step of the way regarding the teaching and learning practices discussed during the revision process. If this doesn't happen, the principal, and consequently the teachers, will never own the teaching and learning process and curriculum initiatives will never translate into practice. The curriculum will be sporadically implemented by random teachers, instead of *all* teachers fully implementing the curriculum for sustained achievement.

Two ways to put teaching and learning first and to avoid sporadic implementation are to (1) develop an organizational structure that allows the curriculum leadership staff to have ownership for principal supervision and (2) make teaching and learning the focus for principals' professional development.

There needs to be a direct connection between the curriculum leader for the district and principals. The curriculum leader should have the most frequent contact with principals, be in charge of principals' meetings and agendas, and play a significant role in principals' evaluations. Principals' jobs are complex, and in order to remain strong instructional leaders, they need support from the central office.

## The Role of the Central Office

The role of the curriculum leader for the district is similar to that of a juggler. Instead of juggling balls, the curriculum leader juggles the demands of multiple curriculum areas and their corresponding instructional issues. Each content area needs attention to stay in the air or move forward. The central office leader needs to engage in three crucial roles to make this happen: the visionary, the gatekeeper, and the change agent.

As the visionary, the central office administrator needs to know *where* and *how* to lead curriculum teams. Before entering into a curriculum revision process, the central office leader needs to have a thorough understanding of teaching and learning issues within a specific content area and have a picture of what instruction will look like after the revision process.

This doesn't mean that the leader has everything predetermined before the revision begins; however, it does mean that the curriculum leader knows how to help the team develop this same understanding and knows what steps to take to get the desired result. The team members will shape the specifics, but the curriculum leader knows the destination.

Providing a vision for the team is a delicate balancing act. Too much vision can feel like micromanaging and too little can make the team feel like they are spinning in circles. Of all of the roles the curriculum leader plays, this is the most crucial, because without a strong sense of what the district needs, it is difficult to engage in the other roles below.

To understand the curriculum leader's role as a gatekeeper, picture this person as a sentry guard who stands in front of each building and classroom in the district. He will allow only effective instructional practices through the gate. The curriculum leader is often inundated with publishers and colleagues who want to implement the latest program of the month. It's the curriculum leader's job to make sure that any program implemented in the district aligns with the teaching and learning goals for a specific content area. It's up to the leader to avoid tantalizing quick-fix programs. Programs won't improve schools; quality teachers who work with leaders to align school improvement processes will improve schools. Well-documented research states that teacher quality is one of the most significant variables that influence student achievement (Darling-Hammond, 1997; Haycock, 1998; Ingersoll, 2003). The gatekeeper will be mentioned more in-depth in Chapter 3 when we discuss data analysis.

Finally, the curriculum leader serves principals as a change agent. After a realistic analysis of the data, there are very few districts that don't have a need to improve achievement in some area. The central office administrator is responsible for identifying and determining how to make these improvements. Obviously, improving achievement will require changes to be made to the teaching and learning processes. Sometimes these are minor tweaks, such as identifying language to teach scientific inquiry; other times, these are large scale changes, such as implementing an integrated mathematics curriculum. Regardless of the magnitude of the change, there will be criticism and resistance. The central office administrator needs to anticipate this resistance and work with the team to minimize negative reactions.

However, no matter how much planning and communicating is done, there will still be a group of individuals that challenge the new initiatives. As the change agent for the district, the curriculum leader needs to stay the course and understand that this is a natural part of the change process. Changing the direction because people may be uncomfortable is not the solution.

We've observed three qualities that separate good curriculum leaders from great curriculum leaders. These include the ability to analyze and question the status quo, the belief that the district can go higher, regardless of district and school test scores, and the courage and conviction to stick with curricular changes until full implementation is achieved.

## Reflections from the Field

When my son Jack turned four, he received a set of Legos for his birthday. The set of Legos he received was designed to be built into a truck. After painstakingly following the directions, I had somewhat successfully put the truck together. Being the highly educated parent that I am, I made sure that throughout my building process I asked my son questions and had him help me find the pieces. However, by the time I was finished putting the truck together, I realized that Jack had moved on to another toy. I was so exasperated. I had spent a good 20 minutes trying to put the truck together, and he wasn't even interested. After taking some time to reflect on the situation, I began to understand Jack's lack of interest. My focus on making the truck look a certain way prevented him from participating in the process of putting the pieces together, which is what mattered most to him. No wonder he had no interest in the final product. Once it was built, it had no relevance to him.

Unfortunately, this same scenario occurs when teams are developing curriculum. In the rush to produce the curriculum guide, we forget that our purpose for developing curriculum in the first place is to improve instruction. The desire to produce a product trumps the process, and as a result we have curriculum guides collecting dust that have little relevance to teachers or students. As leaders, we need to help teachers understand how the curriculum takes the kids where they need to go and show them how to use instruction to get the kids there. We need to ask questions about not only the objectives, but also the methods for helping students meet the objectives.

The next time one of my sons receives a set of Legos, we are going to concentrate more on how to put the parts together, rather than solely on what it should look like. Not only will my boys have more fun, but we all might learn something in the process.

—Ann Mausbach

## Touchstone Texts

English, F. (2000). *Deciding what to teach and test: Developing, aligning, and auditing the curriculum*. Thousand Oaks, CA: Corwin Press.

Jacobs, H. H. (2004). *Getting results with curriculum mapping.* Alexandria, VA: ASCD.

Wiggins, G., & McTighe, J. (1998). *Understanding by design.* Alexandria, VA: ASCD.

# 2

# Aligning the Design for School Improvement

To create real change in this world, you have to have a vision, and you have to have enormous perseverance. It's the same principle that applies in any entrepreneurial adventure: You've got to be too stupid to quit.

—*Marguerite Sallee, CEO, Frontline Group*

## Lining Up the Stars and Planets for School Improvement

Not until Nancy Reagan became first lady did a public figure's use of an astrologer make front-page news and reveal some of the details about this mystical field. After reading a particularly descriptive news article about Mrs. Reagan's astrological consultations, Nancy found a useful analogy for school improvement based on the concept of lining up the stars and planets to determine the future.

Astrologers line up the stars and planetary charts, believing that relationships must be in alignment in order to reveal events and outcomes. If one or more key pieces of information are missing, or if the individual giving the astrologer the information alters the facts, the alignment of the charts supposedly yields inaccurate predictions. While the science of this practice remains a question, the idea of putting facts and suppositions in relation to one another describes a critical but frequently overlooked precept in school improvement.

Many schools and districts expend a considerable amount of time putting plans in place for a mission and vision, data analysis, school improvement plans, professional development plans, and supervising teaching, learning, and people. So, why do schools and districts continue to struggle?

Many school leaders are not lining up these processes to move toward the future. School leaders who learn from misalignment recognize that using one or a few basic processes for school improvement alone will not achieve the power and productivity of combining all the processes together. To understand alignment is to integrate the work; to apply alignment is to predict the future.

## Essential Questions

- What is alignment?
- Why is alignment important to school improvement efforts?
- How do we achieve alignment?

To answer these questions, alignment must be squarely in the middle of school improvement processes. Of all the fundamental precepts included in this book, we believe that alignment is a bedrock principle. Great schools and great districts integrate and align what they do. The payoff is better education for all students.

## What Is Alignment?

How do you know if you have alignment? From our experience, most districts believe they have achieved alignment because, after all, they have data analysis strategies, school improvement plans, and an extensive mission and vision statement in place. They spend thousands of dollars on professional development and execute often elaborate systems for supervision. Isn't that alignment? The answer is—it depends.

Alignment consists of smooth connections between the processes that improve schools and their efficiency. For example, if a principal, a central office administrator, and teachers engage in intense data analysis and develop insights from that work, they can use those insights to influence action steps for a school improvement plan or a professional development agenda.

Another example of alignment could be a team focusing on a component of balanced literacy for professional development. To determine the effectiveness of their efforts, the team would collect data to measure the level of implementation in the classroom and the component's influence on student learning. If the data analysis shows strong implementation and improvements in achievement, the team would return to the school improvement plan and map out their next steps towards continuous improvement.

The answer to "What is alignment?" depends on how the processes are flowing together, how efficiently they work, and how their functions are integrated. Alignment happens when one school improvement process significantly affects another process and makes hard work become smart, efficient work. Alignment is integration, efficiency, and connectivity among the most essential work for school improvement. When the stars and planets are aligned for school improvement, any task associated with one of the blueprint processes can influence another process when the processes are used with a systemic approach. Figure 2.1 outlines the alignment for the blueprint processes.

FIGURE 2.1 Overview of Blueprint Processes for School Improvement

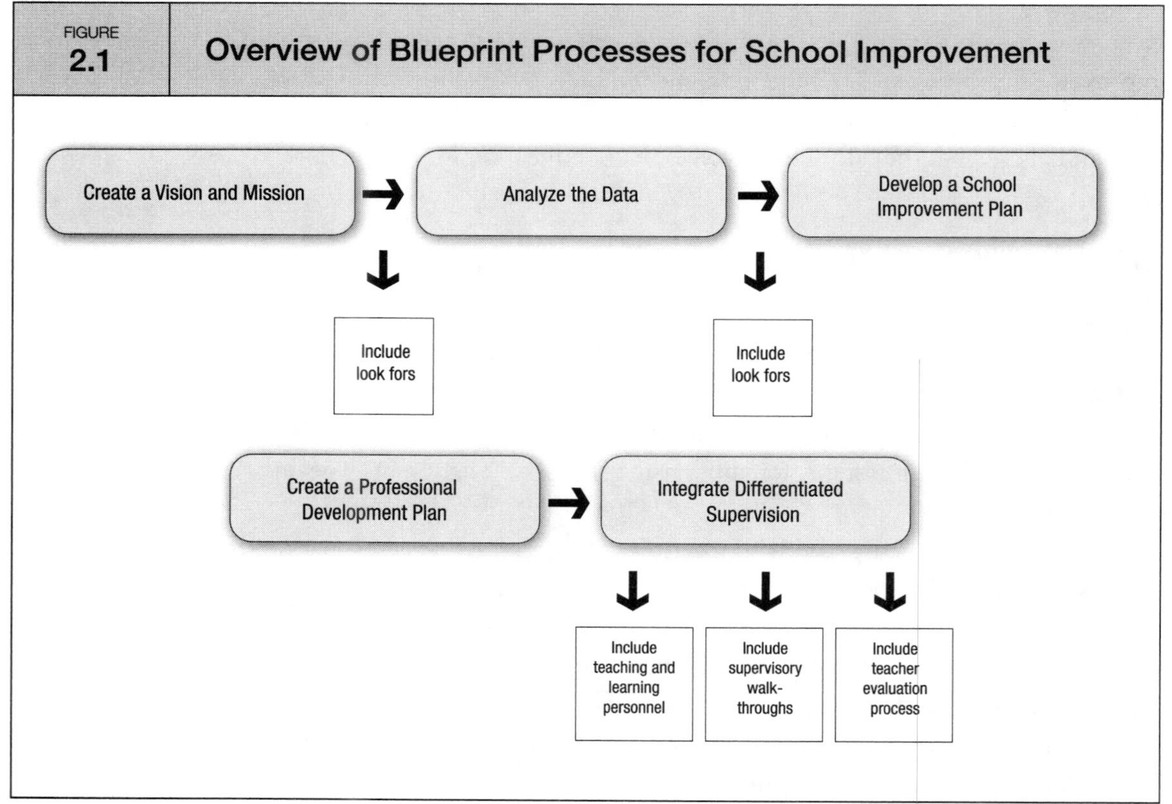

## Recognizing Alignment

So often central office administrators, principals, and teachers take for granted that alignment will occur because of the intense work that goes into analyzing data, developing school improvement plans, implementing professional development efforts, and completing documents associated with this work. Some educators and administrators believe that the effort that goes into each process creates a natural connection between the blueprint processes as a whole. But in practice, we repeatedly encounter administrators who complain about having too much on their plates, too many tasks, and too much paperwork. The result is school improvement without the improvement.

Alignment that works looks like documents that flow together and reference each other. Alignment that works sounds like, "We'll need these data for our school improvement planning," or "Here's some data we can use to document our professional development plan," or "My supervision this year will match our professional development focus." Alignment that works feels like hard work that makes a difference because it is challenging, but not overwhelming.

## Why Is Alignment Important to School Improvement Efforts?

The most important reason to actively seek alignment for the blueprint processes is to make your work more efficient. Lining up the stars and planets for school improvement will improve efficiency to such a degree that this concept will support all of the fundamental precepts discussed in the Introduction.

### Two Heads Are Better Than One

When processes are aligned, ideas flow more freely than when they occur in isolation. For example, a professional development committee at a school meets to outline the focus and substance for professional learning for the entire faculty during the coming year. Ideas flow freely as committee members suggest ways to improve classroom teaching through intense adult learning experiences. Committee members repeatedly refer to data from a variety of assessments as a rationale for selecting a particular focus over another. Everyone on the team is familiar with the school's needs because each task is connected to the school improvement plan and includes references to all the major processes.

This final professional development plan is better because all of the ideas are generated by using data analysis, updating the school improvement plan, and supervising the team's efforts. Two or three heads working together are better than one when it comes to thinking through ways to raise achievement.

### Having a Focus and a Sense of Urgency

An intense focus and a sense of urgency are two additional fundamental concepts that are connected with alignment. Developing an intense focus means placing a laser like emphasis on improvement in one to two areas so that considerable time, energy, and resources are devoted to accomplishing a targeted goal. When the blueprint processes are aligned, an intense focus develops from the work as a whole. Schools and districts with strong alignment readily identify their focus because every process points in the same direction. When the blueprint processes are fragmented and improvement efforts are cluttered, educators and administrators cannot focus on an essential target area with an intensity that is necessary to get results.

When a team has an intense focus on a critical area, the focus inevitably leads to a sense of urgency. Having a sense of urgency to make things better for all students includes actively seeking alignment for all the blueprint processes to help push an improvement agenda forward. Significant alignment flows directly from a sense of urgency to improve teaching and learning for all students. Without a sense of urgency, students who do not benefit from best practices slip away with little more than feigned regret that the school improvements needed for success did not occur during their academic career.

## How Do You Achieve Alignment?

Lining up essential processes to work together seems relatively straightforward. But the practical aspects elude principals and central office administrators unless they subscribe to a few basic practices and beliefs. We caution educators and administrators from rushing into implementing alignment. Alignment requires establishing careful connections between the blueprint processes; this requires more than just producing documents or completing a set of guidelines. Four essential concepts support alignment for school improvement:

1. Embrace the concept of alignment.
2. Aim to use all the power tools.
3. Consciously embed one tool into another.
4. Live by a mission and a vision.

## Embracing the Concept of Alignment

Principals who want to align their school improvement work should start with a serious commitment to connecting each effort. This work cannot be accomplished by wishing it to be so. Step one for aligning school improvement processes is to embrace the belief that connecting the mission, vision, and values with data analysis, school improvement planning, professional development, and supervision leads to efficient and effective progress.

Principals who work in districts where the goals and mission are aligned are at an advantage when it comes to approaching their initiatives. However, just because the district has certain requirements, this does not mean that all schools within the district will achieve alignment in their processes. Even districts with the best intentions to deliberately and intensely seek alignment and monitor how schools complete these requirements will find that only a few schools have structures with real alignment. We regularly encounter schools and principals who approach completing required documents for school improvement as just another piece of paperwork and overlook the powerful reasons for why they should align their work. When schools and districts embrace alignment, two important things happen: for students, achievement improves, and for staff, morale improves because the work of improving their schools makes sense.

## Using the Power Tools

Figure I.1 (on p. xix) lists the power tools that will help you align the blueprint processes. Each tool is explained in subsequent chapters and will assist you with implementing the blueprint processes for school improvement. To achieve alignment, aim to use as many of these tools as possible and select the tools that fit most closely with your current practices. Slowly add these powerful practices and provide professional development for principals on how to use each power tool. For example, you can use the State of the Schools report and the data consultation to improve your current data analysis activities. As these tools become standard practice, it's more likely that alignment will occur.

## Embedding the Tools Together

Consciously strive to use the power tools together. For example, you can embed professional development activities as action steps within the school's improvement plan. Or you can connect the data consultation to help you monitor a school improvement plan or a professional development plan. Using the power tools together increases their efficiency and further aligns your goals. Avoid using the power tools as a check-off list of tasks that must be accomplished. Instead, approach the power tools as a means of moving forward with effectiveness and meaning.

## Living by a Mission and Vision

Alignment means that we are connecting the fundamental processes of school improvement together to achieve a desired school improvement goal. So, why do so many improvement models begin with creating a mission and vision for the school or district?

### What Is Our Mission?

Real school improvement must stand on a firm foundational mission. Embracing a mission for schooling and defining what learning looks like in that school is like pouring concrete into a foundation for a structure. What stands on that foundation depends on the quality of the concrete poured from the beginning of the construction. A fundamental precept for the mission is the belief that the reason that we have schools is for students to learn. In order to achieve alignment, this belief must be more than words on paper.

### What Is Our Vision?

If we believe that schooling is about learning, then what does that learning look like, sound like, and feel like when the foundation is poured and the structural framework is in place? Capturing a vision for schooling clarifies the direction for school improvement work and defines the learning climate, culture, curriculum, and aspirations for the students.

Identifying a clear mission and vision will help school leaders determine what will fit into the improvement processes. However, this will only happen when leaders and teachers live by the mission and vision they create. For example, if the vision for your school is for adults to become lifelong learners through collaboration with other learners, then decisions about professional development would likely include formats such as examining student work in critical friends groups and having a regular collaborative team study. The vision for a school or district should drive the work.

### Using Trifocals

Eyeglasses called trifocals have three lenses to accommodate varying vision requirements. In a similar fashion, schools and districts have three vision lenses.

1. **The stated vision** includes a statement that outlines the hopes and dreams for a school or district as a result of implementing the reform efforts. Many vision statements exist only on walls instead of in the work because they come from futile team exercises or from school leaders who haven't studied what effective schooling is. Certainly, some vision statements represent the beliefs and values of all stakeholders, but more often than not, only a few staff members internalize the stated vision.

2. **The leader vision** embodies what the leader envisions that the school or district will become and sets the direction for leadership activities. Nearly every list for characteristics of leaders includes a reference to a vision or the ability to look ahead to future improvements. Leaders who articulate their vision and align their activities and actions with that vision stand out above the crowd. Visionary leadership is essential to progress. However, having an articulated vision for one's leadership alone is not sufficient. Leaders should repeatedly align their vision with action, reflect on what works and what doesn't, and look to the vision as the guiding light for aligning all the other school improvement processes.

3. **The shared vision** combines the best of all scenarios. A shared vision reflects the collective hopes and dreams of all stakeholders, including leaders, teachers, staff, and the community. A shared vision also includes the leader vision in a statement that everyone understands and embraces. DuFour and Eaker (1998) point out, "If a change initiative is to produce the desired results, [then] educators must be able to describe the results they seek. A shared vision provides them with a compelling, realistic picture of the school they are trying to create."

### Getting the Vision

Sharing the visioning process requires that administrators and educators have a consensus about their values and beliefs and have a clear picture for what the school or district can become. This process can be accomplished by using formal steps and group processes to create a school or district vision statement. The touchstone texts at the end of this chapter include references that show how to create a vision statement.

Creating written vision statements contributes to school unity and clarifies the direction of the work for everyone. Vision statements are valuable and necessary, as long as the effort expended in creating them results in a vision and not just a statement. A vision statement that is created just to be put on the wall or in a notebook seldom drives continuous progress. A vision for school improvement is essential for aligning school improvement. Formal processes should be in place to aid administrators and educators in creating shared vision statements.

Three practices will help administrators and educators develop leader and shared visions. Together, these practices will help you to create a vision that is focused on alignment and will keep your school improvement processes going forward.

**1. Read and study well-known articles and books on effective schools and teaching practices.** A central tenet to creating a vision is studying what already works. You shouldn't take a blank-page approach to creating a vision. If you fail to consider what is already known about producing results, you will only pool together knowledge from you and your staff. You won't see the full picture of what your school or district might become, and ultimately, you will deny your students the opportunity to learn in the best possible ways.

You can start by focusing your study on the best teaching practices for specific subjects, particularly literacy and mathematics. In his book *What Works in Schools*, Robert Marzano (2003) identifies school-level, teacher-level, and student-level factors known to exist in schools that work effectively. He also names other researchers whose work powerfully describes characteristics and practices proven to work in effective schools. This body of knowledge must not be ignored when creating a vision for a school or district. From this book, educators now know what works, and what great schools and strong leaders do that works. The touchstone texts at the end of this chapter are also strong starting points for studying what works.

**2. Reflect and think critically about well-known effective practices and conditions.** Compare your school's or district's current practices to these standards. Reflection is defined as thinking deeply and pondering an idea with the intent to make sense of it in a deeper way; however, this isn't something that only bearded philosophers do. The ability to reflect and make sense of ideas helps to distinguish good central office leaders and principals from great ones.

Moving toward a vision requires that administrators and educators contemplate and compare what is already known to what is possible. Aligning school improvement processes requires reflection that is aimed at figuring out ways to connect various tasks. As a result, learners who are aware of their own thinking can choose better actions that bring results, instead of simply reacting to the first thing that comes to mind.

**3. Talk, debate, and exchange ideas.** Long ago, Piaget (1973) taught us that social interactions can further our understanding. Adults repeatedly cite talking to others as the most powerful part of attending meetings and workshops. Discourse based on study and reflection can galvanize a team and help them create leader visions and shared visions. It is hard to get a vision without some exchange of ideas; therefore, make time for your faculty to exchange points of view without forcing them to make a decision. As a leader, you should wisely choose the colleagues that you talk to and debate with, and you should make sure to stretch yourself to talk with others who have differing views from your own. Visions for the future begin with discussions in the present and reflections on the past. Having open conversations will further your thinking and improve your decision making.

## Mission, Vision, and Alignment

A young, first-year principal once confessed to Nancy that she knew she was supposed to have a vision for her new principalship that emphasized teaching and learning; however, the only real vision she had so far was assigning all the children to a teacher, supplying all the classrooms with materials, and making sure that the buses arrived on time. Nancy's first advice for her was to start with her current vision and to recognize it as an operational and developmental vision for a beginning principal. She encouraged her to apply critical operational skills to create a safe and caring environment.

For this young principal, her vision was a starting point for creating a school that was well-organized, caring, safe, and efficient. She envisioned herself as confident leader who could handle operational matters, resolve conflicts, and build an environment that nurtures learning. Certainly, excellent schools and districts have order as an attribute. Robert Marzano and colleagues (2005) include order in their 21 responsibilities of the school leader and define it as the ability to establish a set of standard operating procedures and routines. But much more is required from school leaders. To keep a vision focused solely on operations for any length of time denies the mission of school as a place to learn. Too often, visioning ends in the minutia of operational details, even when a wider, written vision statement is available.

Nancy's continued advice to the young principal was to actively seek a more comprehensive vision that was focused on teaching and learning. As a central office leader, Nancy's responsibility was to recognize this principal's need for a vision and to assist her in developing it.

Developing a vision for teaching and learning evolves as leaders discover what students need to know, do, feel, and think and as they learn what the school can become. As these pictures begin to clearly emerge, these leaders will be compelled to action. When the vision is clearly articulated, and when the brutal facts about a school's or district's current status emerge, a sense of urgency will develop as people begin to see the gap between their vision and where they are. Edie Holcomb (2004) notes, "The relationship between the mission and the school portfolio is that one should provide evidence of the other." Likewise, the goals for improving a school or district should create an urgency to bring the vision to reality.

A shared vision cannot be legislated, mandated, or imposed. No central office, even with the best of intentions, can infuse a shared vision in a school where there are no common understandings, beliefs, or agreements about its future direction. Many reform models require teams or groups to use visioning activities to develop unity and consistency before the work begins. While we find these efforts admirable, they are misplaced. We believe that visioning should be a continuous process, not a one-time event.

So, is it necessary to have a written vision statement before initiating all the other processes and working toward alignment? Many school vision statements exist without subsequent actions to make the vision come to life in the school. From that perspective, a vision statement is not necessary to begin the work. But from quite another perspective, shared values and beliefs coupled with a clear picture of what the school or district can become spearhead improvement and reform. We believe that visionary leadership from principals, central office administrators, and teachers must be present for great schools to emerge. Without it, there will be no real reform or lasting progress.

In the absence of a clearly articulated vision, start somewhere. Creating a vision is a continuous process; therefore, your time and experiences can help you to shape a clearer vision. Ultimately, you and your team should be committed to developing a shared vision and values rather than just completing the vision statement itself.

Aligning your mission and vision with the school or district improvement plan and data isn't rocket science. We now know the successful educational processes that have become proven practices. The alignment challenge is to make these common practices become common sense.

## The Role of the Central Office

Lining up a school's mission and vision starts with leadership from the central office. Certainly, there are principals who can and do align their improvement efforts without interventions from the central office. But even their best efforts cannot be fully achieved without combining their school alignment efforts with the district's efforts.

To help central office administrators align their school improvement work, we offer the following guidelines from Richard Wallace (1997), superintendent emeritus of the Pittsburgh Public Schools. He organizes his guidelines in a three-tiered approach that he refers to as the focus–follow-up–finish.

### Focus on Alignment

**1. Equip all central office staff and school principals with the knowledge and skills for aligning school improvement processes.** It is particularly important for all central office departments to provide support for schools as they strive to connect their various school improvement processes. Take the lead at the central office level to provide a shared understanding of alignment. Include training on practical steps to develop a meaningful shared vision. Teach your staff the facilitation skills that will be necessary to lead groups as they work with data, create an improvement plan, design professional development, and monitor their own implementation.

**2. Combine professional development on alignment with clear expectations for how schools will align their school improvement work.** Distinguish between understanding about alignment and the practical expectations for how alignment should look in school improvement documents and tasks. For example, as principals align their data analysis with their school improvement plans, they should also have time to discuss how these steps are connected during a data consultation. Without clear expectations for making the processes work together, there is little chance for deep implementation.

**3. Provide multiple opportunities for principals to read and study about effective schools, effective leadership, and best practices in teaching and learning.** Principals who are smart about what works develop schools where every aspect of the school's work aligns with practices that make a difference. Central office leaders must make professional learning for principals a priority. This will ensure that principals are able to align school improvement processes with best practices and current thinking. According to Wallace and colleagues (1997), school leaders who are struggling to develop a clear instructional vision for their work need continuous study time to develop the organization's capacity and to achieve the district's goals.

**4. Teach and model reflection at the central office and in schools. Lining up improvement efforts requires time for reflection.** For busy principals, this time rarely presents itself without initiatives and support from central office leaders. Central office staff members can make efforts to provide principals with reflection time during meetings with reflective exercises, or they can set aside time to meet individually with principals to help them reflect on their school improvement processes.

## Follow Up on Alignment

**1. Talk about alignment in every phase of school improvement.** For example, when state assessment data return and a flurry of data analysis begins, central office leaders should link their conversations about these data to the goals and strategies already in place in their school improvement plans and their professional development efforts. When communicating with principals, central office leaders should remind them about and give them tips on linking one process with another.

**2. Central office leaders model how to make connections between school improvement processes.** For example, for every district-initiated professional development effort, central office staff members need to show precisely how the effort links to district data. Central office leaders need to refer to district improvement goals during school visits and walkthroughs. Alignment is a continuous process. Model how it looks and feels at every opportunity.

**3. Monitor how schools align their work.** The data consultation (see Chapter 4) and the walkthrough (see Chapter 7) will help you follow up on alignment for each blueprint process.

## Finish the Alignment Tasks

**1. Recognize and address alignment problems.** Figure 2.2 identifies common alignment problems in schools and districts and suggests interventions from the central office to help improve these situations. Be courageous, identify the problems, and take swift action before schools and school leaders fall behind and student achievement suffers. The central office should serve schools by providing genuine help when problems arise.

FIGURE 2.2
**Common Problems with Alignment**

| Problems | Solutions |
|---|---|
| • Thinking of school improvement as a linear process | • Use professional development sessions to help school leaders explore how all the blueprint processes work together<br>• Set a starting point for school improvement that is tailored for your staff members instead of using a prescribed set of steps |
| • Using annual data analysis versus continuous data analysis for decision making | • Include data discussions in principal meetings, curriculum work, and teaching and learning monitoring sessions throughout the year<br>• Distribute data as they become available<br>• Analyze and collectively interpret the data<br>• Require school leaders to include multiple data sources in their yearly school portfolios |
| • Developing professional development plans that are selected and governed by persons outside of the school<br>• Creating professional development plans that are loosely related to the school improvement plan | • Develop professional development plans based on needs identified in the school improvement plans<br>• Require principals to be active participants in school-based professional development planning teams<br>• Connect district-sponsored professional development with curricular implementations and mandated initiatives |
| • Using school improvement plans that don't include professional development | • Use professional development sessions to help school leaders learn about standards for effective professional development<br>• Emphasize the importance of connecting professional development initiatives to school improvement efforts<br>• Identify appropriate places in the school improvement plan to include professional development activities |
| • Supervising teachers using daily monitoring methods that are not connected to the school improvement or professional development plan | • Set clear expectations for classroom visits and clarify the purpose for monitoring and evaluating teachers<br>• Set realistic goals for monitoring teaching and learning practices<br>• Provide timely feedback that is not overwhelming<br>• Model appropriate feedback techniques for teachers |

**2. Insist that all schools use the blueprint processes to align with one another.** Don't excuse any school from these processes.

**3. Move to the next level of school improvement as alignment for each blueprint process becomes institutionalized.** Every professional sport today raises the bar for performance by moving the finish line. There was a time when a great finish for the men's mile run was four minutes. Today the world's record is under three and a half minutes. The finish line for the mile is the same distance as it has always been, but what it takes to be first to cross the line continues to raise new levels of performance. Central office leaders can move to the finish line by committing to full implementation of each school improvement process and aligning the processes as a whole.

## Reflections from the Field

Recently, I was at dinner with my two children. They were busy coloring on the commercially made placemats that restaurants use to keep young children occupied while they are waiting for their food. My 5-year-old son, Mark, loves doing the dot-to-dot, and he went to work right away connecting the numbers to see what picture would appear when he was done. He was really enthusiastic about getting to the end, so he worked really fast. Unfortunately, Mark still needs some practice with his numbers, and he did not get all of the dots connected in the correct order. His picture was supposed to be an elephant, but it was a bit distorted. When he looked at the finished picture, Mark asked, "What is this supposed to be?"

Has this ever happened to you? You work really hard during the school year, and you are motivated and enthusiastic about an improvement effort only to find that the results weren't quite what you wanted. You find yourself asking, "What is this?" One of the reasons that school improvement efforts fail is because all the dots aren't connected. Sometimes our enthusiasm and haste can cause us to forget to connect all of the pieces in the school improvement process. Missing or bypassing one of these important concepts will provide an end product, but it might not be the result that you wanted. It is only when all the dots line up that we can get a clear picture.

—Ann Mausbach

## Touchstone Texts

DuFour, R., & Eaker, R. (1998). *Professional learning communities at work.* Bloomington, IN: National Educational Service.

Martin-Kniep, G. (2000). *Becoming a better teacher: Eight innovations that work.* Alexandria, VA: ASCD.

Marzano, R. (2003). *What works in schools: Translating research into action.* Alexandria, VA: ASCD.

Marzano, R., Pickering, D., & Pollock, J. (2001). *Classroom instruction that works.* Alexandria, VA: ASCD.

Marzano, R., Waters, T., & McNulty, B. (2005). *School leadership that works: From research to results.* Alexandria, VA: ASCD.

Strong, R., Silver, H., & Perini, M. (2001). *Teaching what matters most: Standards and strategies for raising student achievement.* Alexandria, VA: ASCD.

Wallace, R., Engel, D., & Mooney, J. (1997). *The learning school: A guide to vision-based leadership*. Thousand Oaks, CA: Corwin Press.

# 3

# Making Sense of the Data

Of the best leaders, when their task is accomplished, their work done, the people all remark, "We have done it ourselves."

—*Lao-Tzu*

## The Principal's Lament

"We have all of these data, but I don't know what to do with them."
"I wish the district would help us use data to make decisions."

After serving a few years in her central office position, Ann asked the building principals in her district for feedback on what they needed from her and her department. Overwhelmingly she heard quotes that were similar to the ones above. She was incensed. Hadn't she painstakingly put together data packets from both the national and state assessments that were administered and included executive summaries? Hadn't she provided colorful charts and graphs that showed trends over time? Hadn't she done several analyses of the district's assessments? Ann was shocked and tempted to resort to blaming principals for being ungrateful and unappreciative of all her hard work. She had clearly handed them the data, yet they were telling her they didn't have the data or didn't know how to use them. How many principal meetings had she used to go over data? What did they expect?

After taking some time to let her Irish temper cool down, Ann began to get a sense of what had gone wrong. Nancy, who had previously experienced this phenomenon she called the "principal's lament," helped Ann realize that by simply "doing" data for the principals, she had failed to look at data analysis as a process or a cycle. Once we approached the work of data analysis as a process and used specific power tools, we were able to help both district administrators and building principals become proficient at analyzing data.

## Essential Questions

- What is a practical cycle for data analysis at the school and district level?
- How do you make sense of all the available data?

These essential questions will frame our discussion about using data to make decisions. Few administrators today will argue against using data to drive rational decision making. Most districts use data in some way, but beneath the piles and files of paper many district leaders have a desire for practical ways to make sense of the information.

## A Practical Cycle for Data Analysis

The data analysis cycle has five phases. It is critical for both central office and building-level administrators to understand each step in this process in order to avoid the "doing data" syndrome that exists in many schools today.

- **Collection.** The first step is to collect the necessary data to help illustrate the current status of the school or district.
- **Organization.** Next, the data need to be put together in a way that is both manageable and meaningful to the audience.
- **Analysis.** Once the data are collected and organized in a meaningful fashion, true analysis can begin.
- **Accountability.** Once an analysis has been conducted, the next step is to determine what action plan will address the results of the data analysis. This is often the most difficult and most forgotten step in this process.
- **Engagement.** The final step in the data analysis process is to help the staff begin to understand the data.

This chapter will address the first two steps in the data analysis process, collection and organization. Some discussion regarding data analysis will also be presented, but more in-depth coverage of this step will be included in Chapter 4. Chapter 4 also explores accountability for using data and engaging staff members in data analysis work. Figure 3.1 depicts the cyclical nature of data analysis and the tools that accompany each step.

FIGURE 3.1 The Data Analysis Cycle

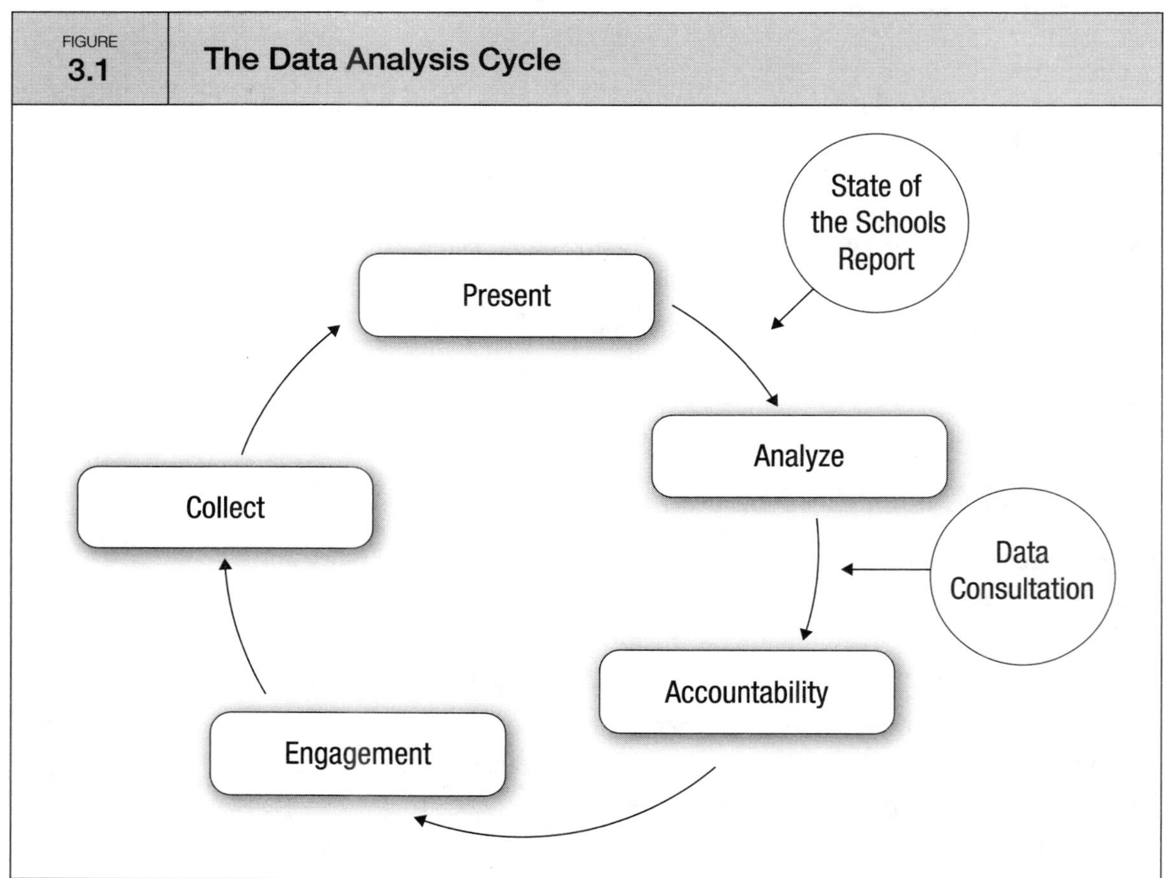


## Making Sense of Data Collection

An essential component of initiating data work is identifying the available data that show the current status of the school or district. So, what data are available? It is a simple question, but one that is often overlooked and needs to be the first priority when you are analyzing data. Two important steps begin the work.

**1. Finding what's out there.** Figure out what data exist. The existing data may give you some insight into the big picture or provide a more detailed look at some of the issues in your school or district.

**2. Collecting the data.** Once you have identified the data, identify how you will gather the information and how you will begin to make sense of it.

## Finding Available Data

To collect the current data in your school or district, we suggest brainstorming a list of your existing data. Most likely you will have state and national assessments that will be critically important to this process, but what other data will help you on this journey? Ask yourself what you want to know but can't answer. For example, do you want to know how many 3rd graders are one or more grade levels behind in reading? What data exist to give you the answers?

In the student achievement section of her book *The School Portfolio Toolkit*, Victoria Bernhardt (2002) outlines key data sources that are helpful in building a picture of achievement. Edie Holcomb (2004) also identifies additional sources for data in her book *Getting Excited About Data*. Figure 3.2 provides a list of common questions to help you begin to brainstorm ideas about what achievement data to collect.

FIGURE 3.2 **Brainstorming Questions for Data Collection**

- What type of information do you collect on a regular basis? Do you collect this information every quarter? Every semester?
- What type of reports does your student information system provide?
- What evidence is available to help principals and teachers understand various levels of student achievement? For secondary teachers, is this information available by content area?
- Which districtwide classroom assessments are administered in your school?

Once you have brainstormed your list, you will need to make a distinction between what is interesting and what is important. A plethora of data exists in schools today, and it is easy to get distracted by data that don't necessarily provide a better understanding of the current state of achievement. For example, high school graduation follow-up data can tell you how many students stay in college after their first year. Although these data are interesting, many outside variables affect a student's ability to stay in school. What might be more important to analyze and collect would be attrition rates for students in higher-level courses in high school.

This analysis may help to determine if the course content and the course sequence are appropriate.

Begin with the data already available and work toward identifying missing data pieces that provide evidence of the district's goals and initiatives. Once you have decided what to collect, you can move on to collection techniques.

Data that are properly collected, analyzed, and presented will intensify your focus on the identified priorities for improvement. A way to determine what to collect is to consider the metaphor of a shotgun and rifle. The pattern of a shotgun shell encompasses a broad area as the beads spread out from the gunpoint. Rifles, on the other hand, send a single bullet at a high speed. A rifle shell goes a farther distance. Using data like a shotgun spreads out the information into thin layers that often fall short of providing enough information to make a well-targeted decision. Short-term or limited data are better than none at all, but they fail to help you back up your decisions with an intense focus. For example, a school decides to collect and analyze large-scale achievement assessment results for a single year. Because the data for even a single school will likely encompass a large amount of information, the unfiltered analysis will be so broad that it won't help the school pinpoint its problem areas, and the solutions remain a mystery.

Using data like a rifle, on the other hand, narrows data collection and analysis efforts to a specific area for improvement. Select a target area and go after heavyweight information that will help you nail down the precise spots where intense work will lead to better results. For example, if a school selected a targeted area such as reading, the school could combine reading data from multiple perspectives and assessments in one intense focus to figure out what improvements have the greatest chance of raising overall performance. Targeted, specific uses of data increase the chances that decisions made from the data will result in actual improvement. Data become valuable when the decisions made from them hit your targets for school improvement.

## Collecting the Data

Knowing what data are available in a school or district is one thing; collecting the data is another issue. Fortunately, technology makes this work much easier. Most national and state assessments include systems for collecting and reporting data that require detailed attention to test security and proper collection guidelines. Data collection at the local level, however, must focus not only on what to collect, but also how to collect it. We share two different tools that are beneficial for data collection in the next section.

### The Spreadsheet Solution

One of the greatest challenges that administrators have is collecting data from multiple entities. For central office administrators, the challenge is gathering information from multiple sites; for the building-level administrator, the challenge is collecting data from multiple teachers.

Nancy encountered this problem when she began working with data in her district. Administrators and educators in her district used an early literacy assessment that was designed to show what students knew at the end of kindergarten. The assessment measured reading skills such as printing letters, identifying uppercase and lowercase letters, learning vocabulary, and documenting early writing attempts. This locally developed assessment evolved as a measure to show the effectiveness of kindergarten literacy programs. Administrators and educators in Nancy's district spent considerable time and energy on providing professional development for teachers, upgrading materials, purchasing equipment and supplies to support best practices, and developing an assessment to measure student outcomes.

Although sufficient technology was available at the time for speedy communication among schools in the district, no systems were in place to collect and analyze raw scores from individual students in the classrooms. The data were useful in the classroom, but data collection difficulties prevented schools and districts from using these measurements for program evaluation.

Nancy's solution was to use a Microsoft Excel spreadsheet to collect raw data from each school for each measure on the assessment. For the assessment, students could score from 0 to 3 on each subtest. Nancy collected the number of students who scored at each level for each subtest on the spreadsheet (see Figure 3.3 for a sample spreadsheet). Her tiered collection system included the following:

- **Classroom level:** Teachers reported scores from their classrooms.
- **School level:** Principals collated information from classrooms to produce a school report that showed the percentage of students who scored at each range for the subtests.
- **District level:** Administrators combined the results to show an overall range for test scores. This particular assessment was administered as both a pre- and post-test for students; therefore, the school and district reports revealed a range of scores for both test periods.

This was not highly sophisticated data work, but these simple spreadsheets provided much-needed information about this assessment. Sometimes less sophisticated methods can help ensure our understanding of data. Simple data collection can have great benefits when it comes to the next step in the data cycle, data analysis.

FIGURE 3.3

## Sample Spreadsheet for Data Collection

Early Literacy Assessment Report
Lowercase Letter Identification 2003-04

| | | | 0 | 1 | 2 | 3 |
|---|---|---|---|---|---|---|
| School A | Fall | Letter ID—LC | 19% | 21% | 21% | 40% |
| School A | Spring | Letter ID—LC | 92% | 6% | 3% | 0% |
| School B | Fall | Letter ID—LC | 24% | 24% | 18% | 33% |
| School B | Spring | Letter ID—LC | 98% | 2% | 0% | 0% |
| School C | Fall | Letter ID—LC | 28% | 15% | 15% | 41% |
| School C | Spring | Letter ID—LC | 95% | 3% | 3% | 0% |
| School D | Fall | Letter ID—LC | 33% | 15% | 15% | 38% |
| School D | Spring | Letter ID—LC | 95% | 5% | 0% | 0% |
| School E | Fall | Letter ID—LC | 33% | 6% | 15% | 46% |
| School E | Spring | Letter ID—LC | 94% | 4% | 0% | 2% |
| School F | Fall | Letter ID—LC | 42% | 16% | 8% | 34% |
| School F | Spring | Letter ID—LC | 98% | 0% | 2% | 0% |
| School G | Fall | Letter ID—LC | 20% | 13% | 18% | 49% |
| School G | Spring | Letter ID—LC | 93% | 7% | 0% | 0% |
| School H | Fall | Letter ID—LC | 41% | 14% | 20% | 25% |
| School H | Spring | Letter ID—LC | 94% | 6% | 0% | 0% |
| School I | Fall | Letter ID—LC | 23% | 10% | 23% | 44% |
| School I | Spring | Letter ID—LC | 89% | 8% | 3% | 0% |

## Power Tool: The Black Folder

The spreadsheets helped Nancy gather local assessment information from multiple sites and create useful reports. As the data work expanded, the number of spreadsheet reports needed to gather the school-based information also increased. To help principals complete these spreadsheets during their busiest time of the year, Nancy gave each principal a black double-pocket folder that contained hard-copy samples of spreadsheets that she needed to gather data. Each spreadsheet included a detailed explanation of the information that Nancy requested and instructions on how to complete the spreadsheet electronically. The hard copies reminded the principals about the required data elements and established uniform standards for submitting results. All the necessary tools for data collection were delivered to principals via e-mail. The double-pocket collection of reports came to be known as the black folder, a symbol of data collection at the school level.

The black folder is a way to both standardize types of data and create a process for collecting those data. The rewards of having organized data in an accessible form far outweigh the difficulty of collecting scores and entering them into a spreadsheet. Districts that already have technology solutions for data collection can simply add their own information and time lines to the black folder instructions. The black folder creates accountability for principals and central office administrators without imposing a "death-by-data" attitude.

### Designing and Organizing Your Own Data Collection System

Using technological solutions for assessments makes data collection almost like a magical experience; complex data are compiled from multiple sites and collated into quality reports, graphs, and tables. But how can you analyze data that aren't collected in a prepackaged technology system? Many small school districts face this challenge, and even large districts with departments dedicated to assessment struggle to collect information and create useful reports for data analysis. One solution is to design a system that collects data in one central location and generates useful reports. The system can be as complex or as simple as the human and fiscal resources in your school or district will allow. Small schools and districts can use hard-copy files or reports as collection tools. Collecting the reports is more a matter of determining what data to submit than devising complex technological systems.

Ultimately, aligning data with your mission, vision, and values requires that you know the current state of affairs in your school or district. From the beginning, it is important to use multiple sources of data to see trends and patterns across tests, grade levels, teachers, student population, and other data sources. When all the data come together, you can see the big ideas and avoid the danger of making decisions based on single sources of information. Knowing what data to collect and how to collect them are the first steps toward making these results happen.

Data analysis can be like looking at a myriad of stars in the night sky. At first glance, the data appear as masses of numbers and singular bits of information. As educators have more training, they can begin to gain insight by organizing the data. The most sophisticated data analysis comes from professionals who are trained in educational assessment. Two tools that we have used successfully to help us organize data are the State of the Schools report and the school portfolio.

## Power Tool: The State of the Schools Report

Each year the president of the United States comes before Congress to deliver the State of the Union address. The State of the Union address has become an American tradition, and Americans expect to hear the president report on important matters and update citizens on any progress made toward campaign promises or other weighty issues affecting the country.

Using the State of the Union address as a model, Nancy focused her data collection efforts on a document titled the State of the Schools. This document is a portfolio containing pertinent data that help educators and administrators have a greater understanding of the teaching and learning initiatives and the student achievement measures in the district. The central office administrator in charge of creating this report must know the data inside out and is accountable for collecting and analyzing the measurements that are the heart of the district's and school's goals.

It is critical for central office administrators to develop this report and not to delegate this task. First, it provides an in-depth understanding of the current status of the school district. This understanding is imperative if administrators want to effect positive change and be proactive in their approach to the work that needs to be done throughout the district. Second, developing this report will provide a model for building principals who will develop their own school portfolios later in the process. When central office administrators develop this report, it strengthens their relationship with building principals and shows principals that they are not being asked to do something that central office administrators aren't willing to do themselves.

## State of the Schools Audience

The State of the Schools report provides pertinent data to the superintendent of schools, central office administrators, and principals. The report is intended to be used for an internal audience, but it can also be used as an external resource for users outside the district. Portions of the report are easily adapted for other audiences, such as the local board of education. Many facts included in your State of the Schools report may be disclosed to the media and the general public; however, your internal audience should have the first look at the facts in your portfolio.

## State of the Schools Content

The State of the Schools report includes data that reflect the district's and school's goals and show how students perform on national, state, and local achievement tests. For example, a goal aimed at closing the achievement gap for low-income students would require data measurements on student achievement in disaggregated forms. In addition to achievement scores, data from staff and community surveys and demographic surveys should be added to the report.

Figure 3.4 provides a sample table of contents for a State of the Schools report for a K–12 district. We produced these documents to focus on student achievement data and information related to the district's goals. Other information, however, could be included to produce an even more comprehensive district portfolio, such as the system outlined by Victoria Bernhardt (2002).

## Content Components for the State of the Schools Report

The State of the Schools report should include an introductory section that presents the district's goals and explains the purpose and audience for the document.

Each data section of the State of the Schools report follows a similar format to provide consistency for the reader. We used four sections as a template for each data piece included in the report. Appendix A (see p. 166) shows a sample using a mathematics software program that includes all four suggested sections.

### Rationale

A rationale or background for the selected data provides readers with a context for the information and helps them understand how to analyze and interpret the results. For example, data for achievement assessments should include background

FIGURE 3.4

## Sample State of the Schools Table of Contents

**State of the Schools Report**
**Achievement City Public Schools**
**2004-05**
**Table of Contents**

I. **District Overview**
- Introduction and Overview to State of the Schools Report
- Achievement City School District Vision and Mission Statement
- Achievement City School District Strategic Plan – Critical Issues
- Achievement City School District Comprehensive School Improvement Plan (CSIP)
- Achievement City Public School Continuous Improvement Model

II. **Demographics**
- Background and Executive Summary
- District Enrollment Trends
- Student Attendance Data
- Free and Reduced-Priced Lunch Report
- Discipline
- Student Mobility Report
- Class Size Information
- Annual Retention Report
- Attendance Area Report

III. **State Assessment**
- State Assessment Background and Executive Summary
- State Assessment Achievement Level Descriptors
- State Assessment Report
- State Assessment Multi-Year Trend Lines

IV. **AYP / APR**
- AYP Overview Report
- APR Overview Report
- District APR
- Building APR

V. **Local Benchmarks**
- **Communication Arts**
    - Elements of Reading Scores
    - Spelling Scores
    - Writing Scores
- **Mathematics**
    - Math Essentials (Elementary Only)
    - District Benchmark by Grade Level and Building

FIGURE 3.4

**Sample State of the Schools Table of Contents** *(continued)*

VI. **Professional Development**
- Background and Executive Summary
- District Needs Assessment Data
- DESE Professional Development Survey Data

VII. **District Survey Data**
- Background and Executive Summary
- District Survey Data
- Elementary Survey Data by Building
- Secondary Survey Data by Building

VIII. **Data Consult / Profile**
- Data Consult Process
- Preparing for the Data Consultation
- Data Analysis Guide
- Data Analysis Worksheets
- Data Consultation Checklist (Quality Criteria)
- School Portfolio Guidelines

IX. **SIP Tools**
- SIP Quality Criteria
- PD Plan Guidelines

X. **Appendix**
- District Testing Schedule
- Data Consult and Walkthrough Schedule

information about the aim of the assessment, how it was developed or selected, key features or components, and a rationale for its use. Assessments with multiple subtests should include a description and measurement for each subtest. Once written, the rationale can be used year after year, provided the same assessments are used.

### Big Ideas

This section presents the big ideas gleaned from careful analysis of the data from the current and previous school year. Written in narrative form, it summarizes the major findings of the report.

### Recommendations

The third section outlines recommendations for action based on the data and knowledge of the district's or school's goals, their progress history, and their professional development focus.

### Data

The reader can examine tables, graphs, or charts at the end of the narrative section to look for additional insights. This section is particularly important when data are presented by the school. Principals need to have the data tables handy to pull out their school's results and to make school-to-district and school-to-school comparisons.

## Portfolio Section for Principals

This section helps principals prepare their own school portfolio, organize their school's data to align with the district's portfolio, and get ideas for presenting data in meaningful formats. It makes school portfolio preparation easier for principals by providing models that match data presented in the State of the Schools report. Principals can refer to this section to get ideas that streamline the school portfolio preparation. For example, Appendix B (see p. 170) shows a condensed version of the rationale and background section of a local assessment with a space for principals to add their own analysis of school data. Electronic copies of the report files are transferred to principals to expedite the writing process. Specific information on individual school portfolios appears later in this chapter.

### Worksheets

Worksheets included in the principals' portfolio are designed to help principals format and display data in various ways. Most state and national assessments include a wide variety of reports; however, even the best reporting systems may not present the data in a condensed and easily interpreted format for a particular district or school. The worksheets clarify different ways for principals to think about displaying and analyzing data from the assessments included in the report. We include simple spreadsheets that allow principals to easily insert their school's specific data. Principals can use either an electronic form or a hard copy of the worksheets (for examples, see Figure 3.5).

FIGURE 3.5

## Sample Worksheets for Principals' Portfolio

**School and State Historical Comparison of Upper and Lower 2 Map Achievement Levels**

| COMMUNICATION ARTS (Grade 3) | | | | |
|---|---|---|---|---|
| | School | School | State | State |
| YEAR | Upper 2 | Lower 2 | Upper 2 | Lower2 |
| 00–01 | | | | |
| 01–02 | | | | |
| 02–03 | | | | |
| 03–04 | | | | |

| MATHEMATICS (Grade 4) | | | | |
|---|---|---|---|---|
| | School | School | State | State |
| YEAR | Upper 2 | Lower 2 | Upper 2 | Lower 2 |
| 00–01 | | | | |
| 01–02 | | | | |
| 02–03 | | | | |
| 03–04 | | | | |

| SCIENCE (Grade 3) | | | | |
|---|---|---|---|---|
| | School | School | State | State |
| YEAR | Upper 2 | Lower 2 | Upper 2 | Lower 2 |
| 00–01 | | | | |
| 01–02 | | | | |
| 02–03 | | | | |
| 03–04 | | | | |

| SOCIAL STUDIES (Grade 4) | | | | |
|---|---|---|---|---|
| | School | School | State | State |
| YEAR | Upper 2 | Lower 2 | Upper 2 | Lower 2 |
| 00–01 | | | | |
| 01–02 | | | | |
| 02–03 | | | | |
| 03–04 | | | | |

### Reflective Questions

A set of reflective questions appears in this section to guide principals in thinking through the various assessments in the report. These questions are specific to the data that principals will include in their school portfolio. For example, we examined the data from a local assessment on reading and developed a set of questions that a school principal might answer by interpreting the data.

There is no expectation that all the questions presented will be answered by a single principal, but the questions provide a model for reflective thinking and deeper connections with the data. For principals without a strong instructional background, this section is critical. It provides a way for central office administrators in charge of this report to be good role models and reinforce their role as a teacher of instructional leaders. Figure 3.6 includes examples of reflective questions that principals can use as they develop a portfolio.

The worksheets and reflective questions together help principals create their own portfolios that reflect their school's values and display data from their school improvement goals. Data analysis isn't about having fancy charts and graphs; it is about using data to make decisions. Central office administrators should provide professional development for principals after they present their first State of the Schools report. This session should be aimed at increasing principals' skills and knowledge of data analysis, preparation, and presentation. Central office administrators should provide these sessions annually to ensure that principals have the skills to analyze school data.

An alternative to creating a State of the Schools report is to develop an executive summary. This document includes the background, analysis, and recommendation sections and provides readers with easy access to data pieces for summary information only. The executive summary works particularly well for central office administrators, board of education members, grant writers, or other personnel who require concise data reports.

## Power Tool: The School Portfolio

An equally powerful tool for data analysis is the school portfolio. This portfolio is typically focused on student achievement measurements. As with the State of the Schools report, principals can use this power tool to develop their own collection of data and to interpret their individual school results. Creating the school portfolio helps principals summarize their school's data, describe their school's progress, make decisions that are linked to facts, and share their data with several audiences.

FIGURE 3.6

## Sample Reflective Questions for Principals

**Questions for Data Analysis**
**State of the Schools 2002-2003**

The following questions are intended as a guide for analyzing the various sections of the State of the Schools report. **Use these questions to prepare for a data consultation.**

1. Read the summary analysis of these data on the district summary page (misc. section in the State of the Schools report) to get an overall view of Anytown's progress in reading, writing, and spelling.

2. Record your school's scores on the SRI on a summary worksheet. Use the models for how the district's data are presented as a starting point for presenting your school's data. What, if any, trends are present?

3. Record the names of individual students who produced a Lexile score in the basic or at-risk range. You can get this information from the alert or performance reports of the SRI. Use these individual student lists as starting points for developing programs of study for students, including tutoring, grouping, and summer school.

4. Note your school's spelling scores in 6th grade. Begin to discuss the Priority Word lists with teachers and students. Aim for 90–95 percent accuracy on this test over words that are most commonly used in student writing. How does the Priority Word list figure into your school's efforts to improve word study? Where will this instruction be given within the balanced literacy framework?

5. Consider your school's writing scores as they compare to other schools. Note the variances among grade levels with each of the three traits that were scored.

6. Look at samples of student writing that were used in the assessment process. Compare the scores for your school with what you see in the samples. How accurately do the scores reflect what you see? What professional development is needed in writing assessment for your school?

7. Consider the results of the CA Survey of Teachers completed by Beth Burchett during the 2002–03 school year. The district results are in the State of the Schools report. Each principal was given the same data for their school. What are the needs of your staff according to the survey? How does that match up with the actual assessment data in reading and writing?

8. Make a plan for each student who was eligible for SB319 and did not attend summer school and/or pass the SRI at grade level at the end of summer school. Work with teachers to develop a reading plan for each student.

One way to develop the school portfolio is to select data pieces from the State of the Schools report and measurements that are directly related to the school's improvement goals. Principals can use the portfolio section of the State of the Schools report as a guide for creating their school portfolio. The sample school portfolio, data analysis questions, and data interpretation worksheets will help principals organize and focus their efforts.

Although it is convenient to develop a school portfolio from district data such as the State of the Schools report, it is not essential. Victoria Bernhardt (2002) provides a thorough framework for developing a school portfolio in *The School Portfolio Toolkit*. She showcases a multidimensional collection of information about a school that includes documentation processes for school improvement. Likewise, Edie Holcomb (2004) describes processes and procedures for collecting, displaying, and using data in *Getting Excited About Data*, an excellent resource for principals as they develop a school portfolio. Additional works cited in the touchstone texts provide detailed explanations and examples of how to create a meaningful school portfolio.

Regardless of the framework that principals use for organizing their school portfolio, it's valuable to have pertinent data on the school's goals collected in one organized document. Creating the school portfolio increases principals' understanding of data and makes them accountable for using them.

## The Role of the Central Office

Collecting data is the thread that binds all the other school improvement processes together. Developing a school improvement plan, implementing professional development, and supervising teaching and learning all depend on data to encourage thoughtful decision making. The central office ensures that the data are sewn into the fabric of the schools and the district by taking on three important roles.

Central office administrators are at the heart of the data collection process. As gatekeepers, they monitor what data are collected, identify who supplies the data, and determine the purpose for each piece of data. If the data are not truly and powerfully useful, they make the decision not to collect the information. Central office administrators stand firm on collecting only the data that are needed and questioning any additional data that creep into the system. The black folder is a practical power tool for this gatekeeper role.

In the role of planner, central office administrators collaborate with principals and other central office departments to determine what data to collect and how to use them. With today's sophisticated data analysis processes, central office administrators should plan ahead to avoid missing opportunities for collecting important data at optimum times, such as survey information or student work samples. Central office administrators who supervise principals can also plan ahead to guide principals in designing meaningful school-based data collections. The State of the Schools report and the school portfolio are practical tools for this planning role.

As facilitators, central office administrators serve principals by helping them prepare their school portfolios. Sending out notebooks, files, and boxes of data is not the same as modeling, assisting, and facilitating the use of data for school improvement. Central office administrators show principals what to do with data reports, provide them with useful templates for data analysis, and teach them how to analyze and translate data into plans for action. They also find ways to make data analysis easier and more productive for principals. The portfolio section of the State of the Schools report is a practical power tool for the facilitator role.

## Reflections from the Field

Most of the time when I figure out and create results for myself, I develop a greater level of knowledge and overall competency than I would if I relied solely on others to give me the answers. I often discover this when I am digging out facts and making decisions for myself. However, there are some days when I just wish I knew someone who had the answers! It would all be so simple.

One day I had spent a couple of hours constructing an elaborate chart of figures to show how IEP students performed on state assessments. After I finished the chart, I discovered a report with all the information laid out in nice neat rows. I could have saved valuable time and energy, but quite honestly, I am sure that I would not have understood the data nor appreciated their value had I not literally constructed the analysis for myself. Now I know what the data mean and how they were derived.

Please don't mistake this insight to mean that we should all construct every piece of data by ourselves and not rely on reports generated by others. Congratulate yourself every time you figure something out or develop an innovation or improvement to an existing form or procedure. In doing so, you are constructing your own learning.

*This is precisely the goal that we want to have for faculty and students. The more skilled you become at creating experiences where teachers construct their own understandings of data analysis, solutions to school problems, and reflections on their own teaching, the more likely their learning will yield powerful and long-lasting results.*

—Nancy Mooney

## Touchstone Texts

Bernhardt, V. (2000). *Designing and using data bases for school improvement.* Larchmont, NY: Eye on Education.

Bernhardt, V. (2000). *The example school portfolio.* Larchmont, NY: Eye on Education.

Bernhardt, V. (2002). *The school portfolio toolkit.* Larchmont, NY: Eye on Education.

Cox, J. (1996). *Your opinion, please!* Thousand Oaks, CA: Corwin Press.

Holcomb, E. (2001). *Asking the right questions: Techniques for collaboration and school change.* Thousand Oaks, CA: Corwin Press.

Holcomb, E. (2004). *Getting excited about data.* (2nd ed.). Thousand Oaks, CA: Corwin Press.

Johnson, R. (2002). *Using data to close the achievement gap.* Thousand Oaks, CA: Corwin Press.

# 4

# Providing Accountability for the Data

In order to be a leader, a man must have followers. And to have followers, a man must have their confidence.

—*Dwight D. Eisenhower*

After a few years in her job as a central office administrator, Ann became concerned that she was spending too much time simply providing forms and deadlines and not enough time on implementing school improvement plans. How could she be sure that the plans she painstakingly put together were actually improving student achievement?

With dreams of fully implementing her district's initiatives, Ann developed what she thought would be a surefire process. Every fall and spring, Ann and the district superintendent spent one hour with each building's school improvement team. At the fall meeting, the building team shared how they used building data to determine objectives and strategies in their school improvement plan. The team presented their data collection systems to provide evidence of implementation. During the spring meeting, the team shared student work samples, portfolios, classroom assessments, and other evidence to show student achievement. At the end of each visit, the central office provided feedback to the team via a rubric that Ann developed to communicate their expectations and to ensure quality discussion.

Two years later, Ann and her team realized that the meetings had turned into a dog-and-pony show. Each year, the same superstar teachers stood up and shared slick, colorful brochures, data charts, and wonderful samples from two to three students' work. What didn't happen was full-scale implementation, as evidenced by the continued flat trend lines for student achievement.

Ann had to move from looking at single, snapshot performances of exceptional teachers to a deeper analysis linked to school improvement and professional development. She knew she needed something else, but she wasn't quite sure what else could be done. Her answer was using the data consultation and the on-site school supervision visits as power tools for school improvement. By using these tools, Ann and her team moved away from the dog-and-pony show and began to monitor teaching and learning at a deeper level.

## Essential Questions

- How do district and school leaders hold themselves accountable for using data?
- How do leaders align data with the other school improvement processes?

Today's principals are faced with the challenge of balancing ever-increasing work demands and their desire to have a life outside of work. What would motivate a principal to spend even more time collecting multiple data pieces, preparing a school portfolio, and analyzing these findings? The essential questions posed in this chapter aim to explore the deep issues of accountability for using data and aligning data with all the other improvement processes.

## Power Tool: The Data Consultation

The data consultation is a scheduled conversation between the school administrative team (e.g., principals and assistant principals) and one or more central office administrators. We generally conduct data consultations in the fall following the acquisition of state assessment data. This is a practice based solely on personal preference. The timing of the data consultation can be justified at almost any point in the school year or on multiple occasions depending on need and data availability. This meeting helps keep principals and central office administrators accountable for processing their data and aligning this information with their school improvement processes. During this session, this group will discuss the school portfolio or data collection system, the school's improvement plan, and the school's professional development efforts. Both parties prepare for the consultation by studying the data and forming questions and ideas to discuss. At the consultation, the principal presents the facts, big ideas, and action steps related to the data from the school's portfolio. The central office administrator listens, asks reflective questions, and offers insights. The school's improvement plan goals, strategies, and action steps are reviewed to ensure that they are aligned with each other and with the existing data. The school's professional development plan is also reviewed to make sure that the professional knowledge and skill-building activities match the school's goals or strategies.

The data consultation also helps to motivate building principals and central office administrators to create and analyze their district or school portfolio. Over the years, we have heard from a number of principals who said that they wouldn't have prepared or analyzed data in a comprehensive way on their own without being held accountable for showing up at their scheduled data consultation appointment. In the end, those same principals express how much they value the process and the insights that they gain from the experience. The data consultation helps principals build the knowledge and the skills for using data and establishes a relationship of trust and respect between principals and central office supervisors.

## Who Participates in the Data Consultation?

While there may be multiple participants in a data consultation, the primary conversation occurs between principals and their central office supervisor or the central office administrator in charge of assisting principals with teaching and learning issues. In order for the consultation process to be meaningful, both parties need to be accountable to one another. For example, if principals meet with a central office administrator to discuss their school's data, improvement plan, and professional development efforts, and then discovers that this information matters very little to their immediate supervisor, all the power of the consultation fades. Principals must have conversations about school improvement with the central office administrator who guides the school improvement process and who serves as a leader for the principal. The title of the central office administrator in this position isn't as important as the relationship that develops between this individual and the principals whom they serve.

As a principal, avoid inviting groups of people from the school who aren't directly involved with the purpose of the consultation. The data consultation is not a show or performance for the central office. Carefully select who will participate in the data consultation. Choose personnel whom you trust and who can build genuine relationships. We prefer a tight-knit dialogue with the school administrative team and one or two central office administrators. The data consultation is an important component for school improvement accountability; therefore, carefully choose who comes to the data table.

## How Is a Data Consultation Conducted?

The data consultation is a conversation where both parties can listen and respond, offer and accept. This conversation is most effective when the atmosphere is conducive for thoughtful exchanges. Typically, the participants sit facing one another at a table with ample space to display the data pieces from the school portfolio, make notes, and share information. Nancy frequently has a flip chart handy to help the participants in her data consultations visualize a particular piece of data or an idea for school improvement. We both strive to listen first, and then ask reflective questions aimed at helping the principal think about data interpretations. The best data consultations sound like two colleagues who are deeply engaged in a conversation about issues of critical importance. Both parties are excited and have a sense of urgency about the topic of discussion. An outline of the data consultation appears in Figure 4.1.

During the consultation, Nancy deliberately applies the technique of reflective listening by listening intently to principals to discern what they know about their school's progress and to gain new insights from their perspectives on the principalship. Without this intense listening, Nancy cannot form the deep, reflective questions that she needs to push the conversation forward. Throughout the conversation, Nancy asks questions that help principals clarify their thinking, pinpoint specific points from the data, challenge their ideas, uncover facts, or ponder ideas to keep the discussion going. She often restates key ideas from her discussions with principals to ensure her own understanding and to allow the principals to hear their insights from another perspective. The reflective listening technique helps to make the conversation at the data consultation more collegial. Figure 4.2 includes a list of open-ended questions to use as models for reflective listening.

FIGURE 4.1

## Data Consultation Outline

I. **Greeting and Purpose**
   - A. Welcoming tone
   - B. Establish purpose for the consultation

II. **Review of State Assessment Data**
   - A. Just the Facts
     1. Gains and losses
     2. Achievement level
     3. Multiyear trends
     4. Disaggregated results
     5. Content or strand disaggregation
     6. Analysis by question type and/or process skills
   - B. The Big Ideas
   - C. The Action Plan

III. **Review of Local Assessment Data**
   - A. Just the Facts
     1. Communication Arts (reading and writing)
     2. Mathematics
     3. Science
     4. Social Studies
     5. Early childhood assessments
     6. Other
   - B. The Big Ideas
   - C. The Action Plan

IV. **Review of Action Plans**
   - A. The Action Plan (short term)
   - B. The School Improvement Plan
     - In what ways do these data match the goals/strategies/action steps outlined in the school improvement plan?
     - What, if any, adjustments need to be made in light of this data analysis?
   - C. Communication with others
     - How will you communicate the results to faculty and community?

V. **Review of Professional Development Plan**
   - A. Review goals and activities for the current year and ongoing projects
   - B. Make connections between data and the professional development plan
     - What activities reflect the needs presented in the data analysis?
     - How is the staff involved in the professional development plan?
     - How will you know if the professional development plan works?

VI. **Thanks**
   - A. Reward effort and time spent on data analysis
   - B. Encourage future work
   - C. See you at the walkthrough

| FIGURE 4.2 | Open-Ended Questions for a Data Consultation |
|---|---|

**Open-Ended Questions for Achievement Data**
- When you looked at these test scores, what patterns did you see?
- Now that you have looked at these numbers, what are the connections between each set of scores?
- Now that you know the results of this test, what are your next steps?
- What does the state assessment data tell you about student achievement in this grade, level, or subgroup?
- What trends and patterns emerged as you studied the achievement data?

**Open-Ended Questions for General Discussion**
- What led you to that conclusion?
- What factors are contributing to your school's success with this initiative?
- Are there any gaps occurring for any of the subgroups in your school? How does your school improvement plan address these groups?
- Tell me more about . . .
- I am wondering about . . .

## The Principal's Preparation for the Data Consultation

Prior to the data consultation, building principals should update or create their school's portfolio and conduct a through analysis of data.

### Update the School Portfolio

Principals can begin preparing their school's portfolio by using the entire portfolio section from the State of the Schools report to build their school's data repository. They can also review the data consultation outline provided by their central office supervisor. These preparations include the following:

- Using the data analysis questions from the State of the Schools report to focus on interpreting and reflecting on the data prior to the data consultation
- Using the worksheets from the State of the Schools report to organize data into meaningful displays
- Reviewing the data consultation outline for key data pieces for discussion
- Reviewing a description of the data consultation expectations to prepare for the data consultation

## Conduct a Thorough Analysis of the Data

After assembling the school's portfolio, principals continue to prepare for the data consultation by creating lists that include facts gleaned from the data, big ideas, or themes from their overall analysis. They can also develop a list of short-term actions. At this stage, principals are often paralyzed by the thought of interpreting and organizing their data. To ease this debilitating effect, we teach principals how to use the following three-step process. An overview of the data consultation process can be found in Appendix C (see p. 172).

**Step 1: Present the Facts.** Joe Friday from *Dragnet* was famous for admonishing his interviewees to give him "Just the facts, ma'am, just the facts." For the data consultation, we tell principals to present just the facts in a clear and concise way. These points include the following:

- Summarizing the information from each data source into a bullet point

**Example:** Thirty-six percent of 3rd graders perform above proficiency on the state writing exam.

- Combining and summarizing facts to show a trend or pattern

**Example:** Scores for 8th grade students increased in the upper two performance levels and decreased in the lower two performance levels for both social studies and mathematics compared with the previous year.

- Restate the facts by using other statistical measures to simplify and clarify the data

**Example:** The percentage of 11th grade students who scored in the lower two achievement levels was reduced by one-half from the previous year.

- Include disaggregated data analysis

**Example:** Sixty-seven male 8th grade students and 77 female 5th grade students took a math assessment; 41.8 percent of the boys and 28.6 percent of the girls scored at the advanced level.

- Report on data outside of academic achievement

**Example:** In-school suspensions decreased by 60 incidents from the previous year. A total of 150 in-school suspensions were assigned to 82 students during the year. These students represent 18 percent of all students in the school. Fighting and disruptive behavior are the most commonly cited reasons for in-school and out-of-school suspensions.

- Include data collected from the school level

**Example:** A spring 2000 survey revealed that 93 percent of students feel that the school campus and classrooms provide a safe environment.

**Step 2: Create the Big Ideas.** Big ideas are summary statements that provide insights into what the data mean. A school principal, central office administrator, or teacher can gain insight into a big idea from looking at facts about student achievement or other areas of performance. The big ideas should be similar to the findings section of a professional research study. They represent the most insightful analysis possible from the given facts and the context of the assessments. Big ideas often lead school principals and central office administrators to the conclusion that more data are needed to confirm a suspicion or test a hypothesis.

The big ideas can be presented with the data facts or shown as a separate list for each data area that is analyzed. Here are some examples of big idea statements:

**Example A:** Results from the state mathematics assessment show that 4th grade students have made significant gains in geometry and measurement. These areas were targeted for curriculum development and professional training during the previous school year. Performance on open-ended mathematics tasks continues to be a concern for more than one-third of 4th graders in the school. Very little professional training has been targeted for this area.

**Example B:** Students from various reading, mathematics, and writing levels completed a survey on using technology at their school. The results showed that students had low levels of understanding for using computers and calculators to accomplish academic work. Students reported that they like to use these tools, but they do not use them for instructional purposes, such as word processing.

**Step 3: Develop an Action Plan.** The action plan is developed by carefully examining school or district facts about student achievement and other performance measures, and then drawing up action steps to target specific needs.

Action steps must be connected to the school's overall plan for improvement. Creating action plans that are unrelated to the school's plan only puts more on the plates of busy teachers and administrators. Small actions such as improvements to curriculum objectives or assessment techniques can be implemented occasionally.

Develop a simple set of short-term actions that are based on the most recent data. Note any implications for long-term actions that point toward a clearly defined trend.

## Developing Action Steps

Determining what actions to take can be challenging for school leaders, especially principals. Here are five basic factors to consider when developing action steps:

**1. Target Individual Students.** Use data to identify and to develop an action plan for students who have specific needs. This type of data can help school leaders focus on assisting these students with programs such as tutoring and individual student interventions. Students who are targeted for interventions do not have to be at the lowest levels of achievement. Instead, the analysis may suggest that students who fall in the middle range for a particular intervention are typically the most productive. To avoid relying solely on one measure, principals should present data from multiple measures to help school leaders determine what actions are needed for individual students.

**2. Align Curriculum to Standards.** Use data to ensure that the school's curriculum matches state and national standards. Many state assessments provide detailed reports on student performance for each standard. School leaders can use the data to pinpoint deficits in specific curriculum strands; however, leaders should be cautious about making sweeping curricular changes without long-term trend data. The sequence and scope of the curriculum should be considered. Data that reveal weaknesses in the curriculum may be the result of the delivery of the curriculum objectives rather than the objectives themselves.

**3. Ensure Full Implementation of Best Practices.** Use data to demonstrate the level of implementation of the best practices targeted as essential for improving achievement. For example, a school implementing a best practice such as a writer's workshop needs to know the current status of all classrooms employing this practice and the students' level of proficiency. Use data to show the level of implementation before creating new action steps. A thorough evaluation of professional development efforts will help school leaders determine how best practices are currently implemented at each school. School leaders should consider the level of implementation for school initiatives that are already under way before creating new action steps from the data analysis.

**4. Align Classroom Instruction and Assessment.** Use data to pinpoint specific assessment methods that are not currently used in daily classroom instruction. Examine student achievement assessments by question type to uncover how students respond to various question types. Encourage teachers to align their assessment practices so that students can experience a variety of ways to demonstrate what they know and can do. Show teachers how to use data to indicate trends in student performance based on their responses to the assessments.

**5. Identify Personnel Concerns.** Use data cautiously when an analysis reveals a certain trend or pattern for a particular teacher, grade level, or department. Data can help address personnel concerns when sufficient and fair procedures accompany both the data analysis and subsequent actions. Data can also identify teachers who consistently help their students to excel. Principals can encourage these teachers to share their knowledge and expertise.

## The Central Office Administrator's Preparation for the Data Consultation

The central office administrator responsible for the data consultations uses the State of the Schools report and other measures to study each school's performance. This process includes becoming familiar with basic facts about the school, reviewing the school's history of student achievement, and recalling the school's improvement plan goals and professional development focus. We prepare for data consultations by engaging in the following activities:

**1. Complete an Individual School Analysis Form.** Create and complete a simple form for each school that focuses on key pieces of data such as state assessment scores. This form provides central office administrators with a uniform and systemic approach for preparing their data and helps them identify key findings and trends that may be of concern. This analysis helps the central office administrators develop a deeper understanding of the needs of each school and will make it easier for them to make future decisions about meeting principals' needs or providing them with additional resources. A sample data preparation form for central office staff appears in Figure 4.3.

**2. Identify Questions.** Develop questions about the school's data, school improvement plan, and professional development efforts. While every question cannot be anticipated, preparing questions ahead of time will give central office administrators a starting point and remind them of critical issues to explore if the principal does not address all their concerns.

**3. Organize the Meeting.** Organize the consultation room so that you can easily retrieve each school's information. Ensure that supplies such as a flip chart, sticky notes, highlighters, and other data aids are readily available. Nancy uses a three-ring binder to organize key pieces of district data that she may need during

FIGURE 4.3

## Central Office Preparation for a Data Consultation

**School** ______________ **Principal** ______________ **Consult Date** ______________

AYP met not met

MAP-CA CA Trend Line

Elements of Reading

UP2

LO2

AYP met not met

MAP-Math Math Trend Line Other Math Data

UP2

LO2

SAT 10 ACT

Survey Data

Other Data Shared

| **BIG IDEAS for Supervisory Walkthrough and Follow-up** | **School Improvement Plan and Professional Development issues** |
|---|---|
| | |

her discussions. She also develops large charts to hang in the consultation room. These charts help her to point out a particular pattern or trend in the district data that may apply to a specific school.

Preparing for the data consultation makes a difference in the quality of the discussion. It is essential for the central office administrator to have more than just a passing glance at each school's performance measures. It is the principal's job, however, to thoroughly know his or her school's information and to provide additional insights.

## Conducting the Data Consultation

The school administrative team should meet with the central office administrator for an hour or more to discuss the school's facts, big ideas, and action plans; review the school improvement plan; and discuss the professional development plan. While this conversation may take place at a variety of locations, we find that holding the data consultations away from the school provides an atmosphere with fewer distractions for busy principals. A general framework for conducting the data consultation includes the following elements:

- Greeting and introduction
- Facts, big ideas, and short-term action plans
- School improvement plan and its alignment with the data
- Professional development plan and its alignment with the school improvement plan and the data
- Summary statements

A conversation should take place throughout the data consultation to help both the central office administrator and the principal reflect on the data and their actions. In general the discussion at the data consultation covers assessment data from the state, the district, and the school. The discussion also links the data to the school's improvement plan and professional development efforts. Each consultation should take on the individual flavor of the participants, reflect their level of understanding about the data, and help them to push their data into action.

The central office administrator guides the conversation, listens to principals' responses, probes their understanding, offers insights, and considers the perspective of the school. The principal shares specific data and big ideas gleaned from analyzing the data, asks clarifying questions, answers reflective questions, and considers the central office's perspective on their school.

The data consultation should help the central office administrator determine what principals understand about the data; discover what principals' plans are for the data; listen to what principals view as the themes or big ideas for their schools; ask clarifying questions to ensure that principals' explanations are clearly understood by both parties; and clarify and think about additional reflections or perspectives that principals will need to take their work to a higher level.

The central office administrator takes note of any issues that are raised during the consultation and identifies any areas that require follow-up such as providing additional resources or addressing topics during a supervisory walkthrough (see Chapter 7 for more information on walkthroughs). Connecting the data consultation with a follow-up supervisory walkthrough combines the effectiveness of two power tools and helps the central office administrator and the principal align both processes to the real world of school and district leadership.

At the end of the data consultation, the central office administrator can ask the principal questions such as "What will you take away from our discussion today to think about more deeply?" or "What are you walking away with today as some big ideas to guide your future actions?" The answers will provide one more clue about the principal's grasp of the school improvement process. Thin answers may suggest that a principal needs more training; deep, insightful answers may indicate that the principal is ready to stretch beyond the basics of data talk. This final check of understanding will help gauge the effectiveness of the consultation.

## After the Data Consultation

Following the data consultation, central office administrators and principals begin to put the data to work. Principals use insights from the consultation to guide their faculty in working with the data and to revise their school improvement and professional development efforts. Central office administrators reflect on their consultations, document their findings, and prepare for supervisory walkthroughs.

### The Principal's Next Steps

After the data consultation, principals are poised to work with their faculty in new ways. Engaging the school's faculty in working with the data must be a top priority for school improvement. If the school's administrative leaders are the only ones who know what the data suggest about improvement, then the entire process loses its power. Until the insights from the data reach the teachers, the level closest to the students, the chance for significant and continuous improvement diminishes.

Follow-up from the principal after the data consultation includes sharing facts, big ideas, and action plans with the faculty and creating ways to engage and involve them in the next steps. Principals can also use a "data day" to get their faculty involved (Holcomb, 2004) or provide activities to promote active discussions about the data (Bernhardt, 2002).

### The Central Office Administrator's Next Steps

Following the data consultation, the central office administrator should pause to reflect on each principal's ability to use data to make thoughtful decisions about school improvement and align the data with school improvement efforts.

Some principals need further professional development on data analysis. As the central office administrator assesses this area, more themes for the principal's professional development will unfold. These themes become the basis for future training activities to help push principals to the next level of competency or to provide more enrichment or extension opportunities.

The central office administrator can also use the data consultation checklist to assess the discussion (see Figure 4.4). This checklist provides space to record follow-up needs such as additional resources from the central office or recommendations for additional professional development. Central office administrators can keep their insights and observations fresh by completing this form immediately following the data consultation. This checklist could become a part of the principal's evaluation to measure leadership competencies tied to the district's specific standards (e.g., ISSLC Standards, research on Effective Schools, and McREL's Balanced Leadership responsibilities).

## The Central Office Version of the Data Consultation

National and state requirements to provide district report cards and other public documents regarding student achievement create accountability opportunities at the district level. Often these are aimed more at public relations efforts than deep data analysis. But where is the deep discussion about the district's data and the reflective analysis needed to push to higher levels?

The executive summary of the State of the Schools report helps central office administrators organize an internal data conversation patterned after the data

FIGURE 4.4

## Sample Central Office Data Consultation Checklist

Principal ______________________________ School ______________________________

Date of Consultation ______________________ Supervisor ___________________________

**Presentation of Data**

_____ Evidence of data analysis aides such as spreadsheets, graphs, and tables

_____ Just the facts presented in precise form

_____ Data organized for easy retrieval

**Big Ideas**

_____ Big ideas identified in organized fashion

_____ Big ideas presented in summary form, not restatement of facts

_____ Big ideas match the facts

**Action Plans/School Improvement Plan (SIP)**

_____ Short-term action plan is reasonable (based on data and based on time available to act)

_____ Collect copy of SIP

_____ SIP goals and strategies match what data suggest are areas of strength and concern

**Communicating Results**

_____ Principal has a plan for communicating data to faculty

_____ Principal has a plan for communicating results to parents and the community

_____ The faculty plan includes active participation in data review and analysis

_____ Faculty are involved in preparing and presenting further analysis

**Professional Development Plan (PD)**

_____ PD plan includes goals and objectives

_____ Elements are complete for each activity (e.g., topic, description, participants, date, time, and cost)

_____ PD activities match identified needs in the SIP and data analysis

_____ PD plan is inclusive of all PD activities and includes a comprehensive look at PD for the school

_____ Principal is able to fully explain the plan and his or her involvement in planning

_____ Faculty is highly involved in PD plan development and implementation

FIGURE 4.4

## Sample Central Office Data Consultation Checklist (*continued*)

**General**

_______ Principal demonstrates command of the data

_______ Principal clearly made adequate preparations for the consultation

_______ Principal demonstrates value for data in decision making and gives examples

| Follow-up Resources | Principal's PD Needs |
|---|---|
| | |

consultation with principals. For example, the superintendent and senior administrative staff hold their own data conversation by asking one or more persons to present the data from the State of the Schools report while other members of the team listen and reflect on the interpretation and implications for the district. This consultation could also be done effectively in small districts, where the central office is one or perhaps two people, by including the principals in a data conversation about the district data led by district staff. The variations are endless. The important point is to have the conversation at a level deep enough to include talk about aligning the data to decisions regarding the direction and progress of the plan for improvement and the professional development efforts needed to fuel the work.

## Reflections from the Field

At a recent leadership meeting, I heard several experienced principals share their data analysis procedures and techniques. Over the years we had all come a long way in terms of our sophistication and skill at collecting and using data to improve schools. But this time I heard something else in those presentations. I heard principals speak openly about how the data were more than numbers on a page. Principals began recognizing that the data are really about serving the people, interpreting their information, and developing and maintaining our relationships with them.

Our effectiveness as leaders depends upon our ability to motivate and move people to improve their teaching and learning practices. We look to many sources to determine what those improvements need to be, including looking at test scores and observing teachers as we walk through classrooms. Our effectiveness with these tasks depends largely on our relationships with the people we lead.

How do we develop relationships? There are tons of books written and talk shows produced on this very topic. From my perspective there are two basic elements: time and caring. Building relationships takes a serious investment in spending time with the people you lead. Relationships are also about caring for another person. It doesn't have to be a best friend kind of caring; it just has to be genuine, sincere, and sensitive to the needs of the other person. Caring about what is happening in the other person's life has to be an important part of the relationship and helps to build trust and respect. It's hard to have a great relationship with someone who doesn't give a hoot about my life. And it's hard for me to lead someone that I don't care about in a genuine way.

How are your relationships with the people that you lead? Take their relationship temperature. Warm? Cold? Lukewarm? Not even on the chart? Effective leaders develop great relationships.

—Nancy Mooney

## Touchstone Texts

Bernhardt, V. (2002). *The school portfolio toolkit*. Larchmont, NY: Eye on Education.

Holcomb, E. (2001). *Asking the right questions: Techniques for collaboration and school change*. Thousand Oaks, CA: Corwin Press.

# 5

# Working the Plan for School Improvement

If we don't change direction soon, we'll end up where we're going.

—*Professor Irwin Corey*

It was summertime, and like all well-intentioned school district leaders, Ann participated in a retreat for administrators. The purpose of the retreat was to review the strategic plan so that they could monitor their progress and plan for the next year. There were four major goals, three to four objectives for each goal, and several action steps for each objective. For each goal, objective, and action step, the administrator who developed the corresponding document presented a verbal update. The last goal in this particular plan dealt with school improvement planning. The administrator in charge of this goal shared information on the number of workshops that were presented during the previous school year, focused on how to fill in and change an electronic template, and finally, with extreme pride, revealed a planning rubric.

A team of administrators, teachers, and teachers' union representatives spent a year developing this rubric that was designed to help school improvement teams self-evaluate their school improvement plans and become accountable for implementation. As the team took a moment to reflect on the rubric, one astute administrator in the room said, "So you mean you could get an advanced score on this rubric and still be a failing school with low test scores?" The answer, believe it or not, was yes. The team had developed a rubric that had nothing to do with student achievement.

Unfortunately, this anecdote is a true story that exemplifies what can go awry with school improvement planning efforts. Given the dismal effects of school improvement planning, why should educational leaders devote any time or energy on a process that has the potential to overwhelm their staff and slow down any real improvements in teaching and learning?

## Who Needs a School Improvement Plan?

Pick up any educational journal or book on school improvement, and it will be difficult not to notice the resounding lament from researchers across the country about the negative effects of elaborate school improvement plans (Fullan, 1996; Kannapel & Clements, 2005; Reeves, 2006; Schmoker, 2004, 2006). According to Michael Fullan (1996), today's complex and unyielding school improvement plans are overloaded, fragmented, and lack any real improvement for students. Doug Reeves (2006) eloquently describes the wide-scale failure of school improvement plans as "the religion of Documentarianism." He says that the followers of Documentarianism believe that with just the right school improvement plan, the right format, or with all of the boxes completed in all the right places, the deity to whom they pray will grant educational miracles.

Research has shown that school improvement plans can be successful when organizations have clear, commonly defined goals (Schmoker & Marzano, 1999) and simple plans that focus on straightforward actions and opportunities (Collins, 2001). School improvement plans are also more effective when they are planned, implemented, and monitored (Reeves, 2006). Instead of school leaders asking "Why should we plan?" the question now shifts to "How do we plan?" and, more importantly, "How can these plans align with the other blueprint processes for full implementation?"

## Essential Questions

- What is the purpose and value of a school improvement plan?
- What are the essential components in an effective school improvement plan?
- How is the school improvement plan monitored and how does it align with the other blueprint processes?

## Power Tool: The School Improvement Plan

Before an organization can improve, it is has to clearly identify the goals for improvement and the purpose of its school improvement plan.

The primary function of the school improvement plan is to achieve full implementation of the district's curriculum and best instructional practices. As mentioned in Chapter 1, a common curriculum with clear, intelligible standards aligned with appropriate assessments is critical to school improvement (Fullan & Stiegelbauer, 1991; Marzano, 2003; Rosenholtz, 1991). The lack of a clearly articulated curriculum hinders improvement efforts and, according to Mike Schmoker (2006), results in curriculum chaos. If systemic improvement is going to occur across the district, all schools must implement the district's standards and grade-level expectations at a high level. High implementation will lead to more coherence across the curriculum and will level the playing field for all learners in the district.

The school improvement plan is the power tool that helps school leaders fully implement the district's teaching and learning initiatives. One of the fundamental precepts of school improvement is that the work is not finished until every child benefits from the innovations. Without a school improvement plan, this goal cannot be accomplished. The common ground for all schools within an organization is the district's curriculum and instruction. The focus areas for individual schools are articulated through individual school improvement plans. Once the plan has been established, each school can focus on its unique student and teacher learning needs. Figure 5.1 outlines effective and ineffective practices associated with school improvement planning.

### Essential Components for a School Improvement Plan

Research indicates that the most effective school improvement plans are simple and straightforward (Fullan & Stiegelbauer, 1991; Joyce, Wolf, & Calhoun, 1993; Labovitz, Sang Chang, & Rosansky, 1993). To create a clear and concise plan, school leaders need to answer the following questions:

- What **goals** do we need to take us where we are going?
- What **strategies** will we need to get there?
- What **action steps** will help us get the work done?

To answer these questions, a school leader has to understand and distinguish the difference between these critical components.

| FIGURE 5.1 | **Effective and Ineffective Plans for School Improvement** |
|---|---|
| **School Improvement Plans That Don't Work** | **School Improvement Plans That Work** |
| The principal writes the school improvement plan alone or with a few teachers. At best, the school staff rubber stamps the plan. | The school improvement plan is developed with input and agreement from a large sector of the school staff. |
| Each school uses its own vocabulary for writing the plan. Planning sessions are used to determine the format for the plan and to decipher each term and component. | The school agrees to use common language and a common template for the school improvement plan before planning efforts begin. All principals and central office staff members know and use the same vocabulary and definitions for the school improvement plan. |
| The primary goals in the plan are not focused on student achievement and better teaching and learning. | The school improvement goals are focused on improving teaching and learning. |
| School improvement goals are not measurable or attainable. Goals change every year whether they are accomplished or not. | School improvement goals are SMART and designed for a 3-to-5-year period. Monitoring and implementation processes are established so that schools know they are accountable for accomplishing their goals. |
| School improvement goals are only loosely linked to district initiatives for implementing the curriculum. | School improvement goals are linked to the district's curriculum initiatives. |
| There are little or no professional development efforts to support the changes outlined in the school improvement plan. | School improvement plans include professional development efforts as a means for accomplishing the goals. |
| The plan is only reviewed annually and rarely referred to throughout the year. | School improvement plans are reviewed throughout the year by principals, teacher-leaders, and central office supervisors. |
| No one believes that the school improvement plan is the primary plan for school improvement. | The school improvement plan is the primary plan for improving the school's academic achievement. |

## Goals for the School Improvement Plan

Goals are dreams with deadlines.

—*Diana Scharf Hunt*

A meaningful goal is clearly and concisely written and successfully communicated without jargon or slogans. A goal is useful when it is measurable, provides a clear sense of direction, and leads a team toward accomplishing its vision and mission. When goals are accomplished, three important things happen: student achievement improves, schools become better, and the improvements can be measured. To be effective, goals must be SMART:

**S**pecific and strategic: goals are clearly articulated and clarify the vision
**M**easurable: goals are clearly measurable
**A**ttainable: goals are possible to achieve
**R**esults-oriented: goals are focused on the outcome
**T**ime-bound: goals are achieved in a certain time period

Goals written in this manner provide tangible targets. Goals that include broad-based terms to describe the behavior that needs to be changed or improved can be used with diverse populations to establish reasonable criteria for success and serve as the foundation for school improvement plans. Three guiding questions help to determine whether the goal statement will lead to action:

- Does this statement identify the behavior that needs to be improved?
- Does this statement indicate a standard or criteria for acceptable performance?
- Does this statement tell the conditions under which the behavior will occur?

To illustrate the difference between effective and ineffective goal statements, we will use the guiding questions to evaluate the following two examples.

**Example A.** By June 2008, students will improve the quality of their writing by using better organization techniques, and they will demonstrate their improvement by scoring at least 3 out of 6 each trimester on the schoolwide writing prompt.

**Example B.** Students will improve writing by using the 6-trait approach.

**Does the statement identify behavior that needs to be improved?** Both examples identify writing as the behavior for improvement. Example A, however, identifies what behavior needs to be changed. Behavior cannot improve if it is not clearly defined for both students and teachers. Broad goal statements are often one of the major stumbling blocks of school improvement plans. Time invested in narrowing the focus will help teachers achieve their goals.

**Does this statement indicate a standard or criteria for acceptable performance?** Although example B states that the 6-trait approach will be used to measure acceptable performance, the goal statement does not provide criteria for acceptable performance. Will students improve their writing using a holistic score or just one trait? Is there a level of performance that is deemed satisfactory or is any improvement acceptable? These are the types of questions that need to be answered. Example A clearly shows that students need to receive a score of 3 or better to meet this goal. When the target behavior is clearly identified, it is much easier to pinpoint what is and what isn't acceptable performance.

Goals can be assessed in a variety of ways. It may be necessary to measure the same thing in different ways or to use several measurements to show progress. Figure 5.2 provides different methods for measuring acceptable performance. The key is to make sure that the target behavior is being measured. Without appropriate measurements, teachers will not be able to determine if their strategies are helping students improve and school leaders won't be able to proactively analyze student performance and make decisions based on student data.

FIGURE 5.2 **Measuring Effective Performance**

| Measuring Method | Example |
|---|---|
| Time | • Student will be able to run the 100-yard dash in 14 seconds. |
| Number | • Student will be able to identify at least 40 bones in the human skeleton.<br>• All African American boys in 6th – 9th grade will have an adult and peer mentor. |
| Percentage | • At least 85% of students in 5th grade will be proficient or advanced in mathematics based on state assessments.<br>• Less than 5% of all students will have scores in the below basic category on the state assessment.<br>• 95% of 2nd grade students will be reading within Developmental Reading Assessment (DRA) grade-level range.<br>• There will be a 20% increase in the number of students who qualify for college credit based on AP exams.<br>• The number of students who leave school before graduation will decrease by 50% over the next three years. |

Many times, we have heard teachers say that the targeted areas for improvement are intangible and cannot be evaluated. When a school takes on an initiative that cannot be evaluated, school leaders are unable to demonstrate what they are doing to help students. If an initiative is worthy of teacher and student time, school leaders must insist that teachers measure it in some tangible way.

**Does this statement tell the conditions under which the behavior will occur?** It is clear from the goal statement in example A that students will need to improve their writing each trimester by organizing their work and demonstrating their skills on the schoolwide writing prompt. Example B does not provide any conditions for improvement or reveal when and how students will show their improved writing skills. Example B doesn't address these conditions and leaves too many factors open to interpretation for teachers and students.

For further examples of goal statement templates, refer to the touchstone texts at the end of this chapter.

## Effective Strategies for School Improvement Plans

Strategies are intellectually simple; their execution is not.

—*Lawrence Bossidy*

Look up the word strategy in a thesaurus and the following words are included: plan, approach, tactic, and line of attack. Strategies in the school improvement document are the tactics that the team will use to accomplish the goal. While the purpose of the goals in the school improvement plan is to identify the desired outcome, strategies are designed to help determine the line of attack for accomplishing the goals. Schools and districts that desire sustained improvement need to understand the difference between a goal and a strategy. Without an understanding of this concept, school improvement plans will be fragmented. Straightforward strategies that will help school and district leaders achieve their goals are critical to an effective plan. Figure 5.3 outlines the critical differences between goals and strategies. Three key questions will help school leaders develop effective strategies:

- Is the strategy a short-term statement that describes what must be done to meet the goal?
- Will the projects proposed in the strategy help school leaders complete the goal?
- Do the strategies outline every step in the process? (If so, these are action steps, not strategies.)

FIGURE 5.3 **Comparing Goals and Strategies**

| | Goals | Strategies |
|---|---|---|
| **Purpose** | • Identifies the end result | • Identifies methods that will achieve the end result |
| **Questions Addressed** | • What behavior?<br>• Which conditions?<br>• What is the targeted criteria? | • What are the strategic ways to improve or decrease the targeted behavior? |
| **Ratio** | • Uses one goal | • Uses a variety of strategies (typically 3–5) to accomplish the goal |
| **Focus** | • Focuses on outcomes | • Focuses on necessary inputs to achieve outcome |

Using the writing goal that was presented earlier, the following example shows effective strategies for achieving the goal.

**Goal:** By June 2008, students will improve the quality of their writing by using better organization techniques and demonstrating their improvement by scoring at least 3 out of 6 each trimester on the schoolwide writing prompt.

**Strategy:** Increase the amount of writing in all content-area classes
**Strategy:** Implement a writer's workshop for students
**Strategy:** Develop constructed-response assessments for all content-area classes

Notice that these strategies are initiatives that will lead to improvement in student achievement and help teachers focus on schoolwide implementation of the initiative. As school improvement teams begin developing strategies, it is important not to confuse them with a goal or an action step. By using the guiding questions presented in this chapter, the school improvement team can begin to understand the difference and plan accordingly. Consider the four statements below. Which are goals and which are strategies?

1. Implement James Comer's school development model.
2. Increase the number of students who are proficient in science skills and concepts on the state assessment.
3. Establish professional learning communities for teachers.
4. Increase contact time for students who are one year below grade level in reading and mathematics through after-school tutoring and advisement periods with teachers.

Statements 2 and 4 are goals that identify the desired behavior, criteria, and conditions for the change desired in a school. Statements 1 and 3 are strategies that will help school leaders attain their goals. A clear understanding of the difference between goals and strategies is necessary if a school wants to have real, measurable, sustainable improvement for all students.

As school leaders develop strategies, it's important to remember not to take on too many initiatives at once. As Margaret Carthy said, "Be like a postage stamp: stick to one thing until you get there." Keep in mind that the essential fundamental precept for school improvement is to have every child benefit from the improvement initiatives. Keeping this in mind as plans are developed will help to ensure that plans do not become too cumbersome.

Another important consideration for school leaders as they identify and implement school improvement strategies is not to reinvent the wheel. Many districts identify clear instructional models and spend considerable time and energy providing professional development and resources to ensure that these models are used throughout the district. School leaders should not feel like their team has to develop new strategies or ideas that are not well researched or already part of the district's focus. For example, if a writer's workshop is part of the district's instructional delivery model, the building team only needs to identify which aspects of the writer's workshop need to be a part of the school improvement plan. The team's aim is to fully implement the curriculum delivery models that have been approved by the district. Inventing new curriculum is not necessary if the district has high-quality curriculum and learning practices in place.

The importance of having a strong curriculum (as discussed in Chapter 1) becomes more apparent as school leaders develop their school improvement plans. Without strong curriculum and instruction practices in place, the process for developing school improvement plans becomes much more arduous.

## Action Steps for the School Improvement Plan

Plan the work, and work the plan.

—*Ann's Dad*

In an effective school improvement plan, the action steps help school leaders work their plan. Action steps define the strategy and make it easier for school leaders to determine what actions, activities, and resources are needed to implement the strategy.

Using the same goal and strategy from our previous example, we have now added accompanying action steps that are specifically aligned with these initiatives.

**Goal:** By June 2008, students will improve the quality of their writing by using better organization techniques and demonstrating their improvement by scoring at least 3 out of 6 each trimester on the schoolwide writing prompt.

**Strategy:** Develop constructed-response assessments for all content-area classes

**Action Step:** Train staff to develop effective assessment strategies

**Action Step:** Develop rubrics for constructed responses for each content area

**Action Step:** Set up monthly team meetings to review and score student responses on assessments

As the action steps are developed, school leaders should include resources and time frames to help their school improvement teams complete their strategies. It's also important not to weigh down the document that includes the action steps with cumbersome, minute details. Use simple tables to organize the information. Appendix D (see p. 177) provides an example of a school improvement template with action steps and time lines.

As the saying goes, timing is everything, and that certainly holds true for school improvement planning. One of the reasons that many school improvement plans fail is that they include unrealistic time lines. Far too often, school leaders have great planning sessions and develop grand ideas, but those initiatives never fully develop because the principal and the faculty are tied to time lines that are not feasible. It's not reasonable for a school improvement team to do all of their action steps in the first or second year. Instead, these teams need to determine how their actions can be spaced over time. Many forms for school improvement plans include a monthly time line that allows each school to predict when each action will be initiated and completed. Unexpected circumstances may require the team to shift the plan; however, the time line should provide overall guidelines for organizing the work. Staff members can also use the school improvement plan to develop a time line for professional development activities.

## How Is the School Improvement Plan Monitored and Aligned with Other Blueprint Processes?

Plans without monitoring are little better than wishes upon stars.

—*Doug Reeves*

We often relate monitoring school improvement efforts to the messy and complex nature of parenting. Most parents know that constant and consistent messages have the most impact on their kids. It would be preposterous for parents to think that they would only have to tell their children not to fight with their siblings or to do their homework one time. Parents know that if they want their children to do important tasks, like study for a test or clean their rooms, they have to monitor and reinforce their behavior frequently, provide constant feedback, and model the behaviors that they want them to exemplify. Parents also know that while it's important to use formal methods to monitor their child's progress, such as reviewing a report card or attending a parent-teacher conference, it is also important to use frequent informal methods with their child, such as daily interactions, observations, and discussions to give them insight in to what their child needs next.

For school leaders, frequent informal measures coupled with formal milestones help them to monitor their school improvement plans. Just as it would be ludicrous for parents to redirect their children only once a month, school leaders also need frequent check-in points to monitor their school improvement efforts. Three processes that will help school leaders monitor their school improvement plans include:

1. **The Data Consultation.** Central office administrators and principals use the data consultation as a power tool to review and monitor the school improvement plan and to ensure that the most pertinent student achievement issues are addressed in each school's improvement efforts (see Chapter 4 for more discussion).

2. **The Walkthrough.** The walkthrough helps principals monitor teaching and learning practices in the school. This power tool adds accountability to the school improvement plan because it encourages principals to go out and find real evidence of school improvement (see Chapter 7 for further discussion).

3. **The Professional Development Plan.** This professional development plan is designed to help teachers carry out the initiatives identified in the school improvement plan. The evaluation of this power tool at the highest levels is student learning (see Chapter 6 for more discussion).

Monitoring the school improvement plan helps school leaders align the blueprint processes. Many schools and districts never reach full alignment because they treat the school improvement plan as an end product instead of a continually ongoing process. The power tools listed above are the link to implementation and ultimately alignment. They are the power source for the plan. Aligning school improvement efforts can be difficult, but it is not impossible with these tools.

Reflection is another important process for monitoring. Reflection provides leaders with the opportunity to think in more detail to generate new knowledge (Moon, 2005). Instructional leaders must take the time to review and reflect on the school improvement plan. Figure 5.4 provides a list of reflective questions for district and school leaders.

## The Role of the Central Office

The central office administrator helps school principals with their school improvement plans by serving as a teacher, monitor, and role model.

As a teacher, the central office administrator has the responsibility to teach building principals about instruction and leadership. One of the most common problems with school improvement plans is that they do not address the school's instructional needs. The central office leader must work with building principals to help them identify and implement powerful instructional strategies.

| FIGURE 5.4 | **Reflective Questions for Monitoring the School Improvement Plan** |
|---|---|
| • Do the objectives match the school's data? | |
| • Do the objectives support the district vision for improving instruction? | |
| • Do the strategies reasonably accomplish the objective?<br>• If the school fully implements this strategy, would the objective be accomplished? | |
| • Do the action steps also support the strategies?<br>• Are they reasonable in both scope and sequence? | |
| • Does the proposed timeline seem reasonable?<br>• Could a school reasonably accomplish the action steps in the coming year?<br>• Can those action steps be accomplished sufficiently in that timeframe? | |
| • How will the school know when the objective is accomplished? The strategy? The action step? | |
| • How involved are the faculty members in developing the plan? | |
| • Is this an authentic working plan or a document to fulfill requirements of the district? | |
| • Can this plan be used for professional development efforts? | |
| • Can leaders use this plan for differentiated supervision to help teachers improve instruction? | |
| • Does this plan offer a hope for improved academic achievement for this school? | |

The primary function of the school improvement plan is to fully implement the district curriculum and the best instructional practices. This task becomes difficult if building principals are not aware of what these principles are. Principals must know what the curriculum is and how to implement it in order to develop plans that align with district practices. Central office administrators must spend considerable time working with principals to help them understand what instructional practices look like in classrooms. To accomplish this goal, central office administrators can use principals' meetings to help principals learn about teaching and learning rather than discussing items that would be better addressed in a memo or an e-mail. The central office administrator can either deliver professional development sessions on a specific topic or facilitate the process so that other leaders or consultants can provide in-depth training for building principals and other school leaders.

In addition to teaching principals about curriculum and instruction, central office administrators also need to teach principals how to develop an effective school improvement plan and a well-aligned professional development plan. To help school leaders make this connection, central office administrators have to teach and plan time for collaboration and reflection to help these leaders learn the basic precepts of school improvement planning. These discussions need to be focused on how building principals can lead their staff to fully implement the goals of the plan.

Another major role for central office administrators is to monitor school leaders to ensure that they are implementing their school improvement plans. Central office administrators need to prioritize their time so that they are helping principals become fully engaged in practices that will promote teaching and learning. The data consultation, the professional development plan, and the supervisory walk-through will aid central office administrators in monitoring school improvement plans. Although these processes take considerable time, without them, the job of improving student achievement at the district level is almost impossible.

Finally, central office administrators need to provide building principals with a model for what good planning looks like by developing and implementing a district-level improvement plan and by sharing their progress. Central office leaders should share components of the district's plan that are similar to a school's improvement plan, providing building leaders with a visual for their plans and conveying to principals that they are partners in their improvement processes. Far too often the central office administrator is viewed as being too far removed from the day-to-day demands of running a building. The blueprint processes promote the fundamental precept that central office administrators are available to support and provide a vision for school leaders in the district. Providing a district plan and modeling the process coveys the message that everyone is in this together.

## Reflections from the Field

*School improvement work is messy business. As much as we try to make it linear, it simply isn't. It is a circular process that can be both rewarding and frustrating. Nancy relates school improvement to the analogy of lining up the stars and the planets in Chapter 2. How much more complex can you get? I can think of one other thing that most of us do that is just as complex—parenting.*

*As a parent, your job is never done. You have to constantly adjust your techniques based on the needs and ages of your children. You* also have to be agile to adjust to last-minute changes and emergencies. For example, you can have everything planned for a smooth morning (you can even iron your clothes and prepare your lunch the night before!) only to wake up and find out it is costume day and your child needs a Batman mask! Sometimes you feel that you are making progress, only to find your child reverting to old behaviors. Through it all, you learn and grow even when you make mistakes.

School improvement, just like parenting, is about focusing and following through on your plans. It's also about collaborating with and empowering your staff. As you work with your staff, remember how messy this business can be. Be prepared for the unexpected, and be open as your staff members reveal new ideas that you may have never thought of before. Give yourself a moment to take a step back if necessary. Remember, this is messy business, but it also has rewards.

—Ann Mausbach

## Touchstone Texts

Bernhardt, V. L. (2002). *The school portfolio toolkit*. Larchmont, NY: Eye on Education.

Holcomb, E. (2001). *Asking the right questions: Techniques for collaboration and school change*. Thousand Oaks, CA: Corwin Press.

Reeves, D. B. (2006). *The learning leader: How to focus school improvement for better results*. Alexandria, VA: ASCD.

Schmoker, M. (2001). *The results fieldbook: Practical strategies for dramatically improved schools*. Alexandria, VA: ASCD.

Schmoker, M. (2006). *Results now: How we can achieve unprecedented improvement in teaching and learning*. Alexandria, VA: ASCD.

# 6

# Developing Powerful Professional Development

Man's mind once stretched by a new idea never regains its original dimension.

—*Oliver Wendell Holmes*

In Nancy's district, professional development for improving teaching practices once followed a familiar pattern. A published curriculum guide, along with its accompanying materials, was distributed and launched during a district-sponsored training session for teachers. Occasionally, consultants from the publishing company visited schools to provide additional support. Next, staff members from the district office made presentations about the curriculum and answered questions during grade-level meetings for elementary school teachers in the district. Principals attended these sessions, but they did not participate or lead them. Afterward, members of the curriculum writing team who were thoroughly familiar with the new curriculum goals assisted fellow teachers or made brief talks at a faculty meeting. Principals were given copies of the new guides and attended meetings and short presentations about the new curriculum and its accompanying materials. No one at the school monitored how the curriculum was taught, watched how the materials were used to support the curriculum, or collected hard data outside of state test scores to show that students were learning.

Later, curriculum specialists from the district valiantly attempted to help school leaders implement the new curriculum with workshops and after-school meetings. But in a large district, specialists were quickly overwhelmed by working with several hundred teachers at multiple sites. A few enlightened principals attempted school-level professional training. This was not discouraged, but neither was it supported with money or technical advice.

Meanwhile, professional training for teachers continued throughout the district with a potpourri of topics selected from surveys given to all K–12 teachers. Many of those topics were only loosely or vaguely connected to implementing the curriculum goals. At the end of training sessions, participants were asked to complete an evaluation of the session that only rated the presenter, the training room, and their overall reactions to the topic.

These conditions existed as Nancy began her tenure as a central office administrator. Her early visits to classrooms confirmed that the curriculum goals neatly bound in guides seldom appeared in daily classroom teaching. Even materials purchased to support new curriculum remained unused, or they were used without regard to teaching objectives. She quickly learned the difference between intentions for teaching and learning and the reality of classroom practice. The need for professional development to support the teaching of quality curriculum for all students emerged from this experience and shapes the concepts of this chapter.

Although dismal and painful to write, the opening scenarios show scenes that continue to repeat themselves in schools and districts throughout the country. Mike Schmoker (2006) uncovered similar findings when he visited classrooms in several states. He believes that the experience of discovering the alarming gap between reality and our assumptions about the general quality of classroom practice provides the essential starting point for improvement.

## Essential Questions

Fortunately for the students in Nancy's district, greatly improved practices now exist as a result of seeking answers to three essential questions. Connecting the answers to these questions turns teacher training into professional learning with a tremendous influence on student achievement.

- What is effective professional development, and how is it achieved?
- How do we know if professional development makes a difference for teaching and learning?
- What is the role of district and school leaders in professional development?

The good news for schools today is that we know what effective professional learning looks like, sounds like, and accomplishes for both school staff members and students. Five actions help school leaders put this work into action.

1. Develop high standards that will serve as a framework for all professional development.
2. Use models that have been proven to make a difference for adult learning.
3. Connect content from professional development sessions with clear expectations for how innovations should be implemented in the classroom.
4. Have high expectations for teachers and monitor them to ensure that they are fully implementing proven practices.
5. Evaluate and determine the value of the professional learning sessions.

## Developing High Standards

In 1994, the National Staff Development Council (NSDC) set out to develop national standards for professional learning. The current NSDC standards (NSDC, 2001) are grounded in research that documents the connection between staff development and student learning. Twelve standards are organized in a three-tiered schema that emphasizes context standards (i.e., the system or culture for adult learning); process standards (i.e., how professional learning takes place); and content standards (i.e., the knowledge and skills needed to teach so that students learn). A more detailed description for each standard can be found on the NSDC's Web site at www.nsdc.org.

These national standards set a high bar for adult learning that is aimed at improving student achievement. They are practical for judging the quality of professional development activities, plans, and goals, and they help to build a common knowledge base among administrators and teachers for the best practices in professional development. As district and school leaders make plans for professional development initiatives and projects, the NSDC standards are a good framework to reference for creating professional development that actually changes classroom practice.

These standards will help central office leaders and school staff members monitor the quality of both district and school improvement plans. For example, during the data consultation, the central office supervisor and principal review the school professional development plan in relation to data about student performance. The NSDC standards will help both leaders shape criteria for assessing the quality of the school improvement plan and shift the school's professional development initiatives to meet higher standards of effectiveness. Linking the NSDC standards to a school's professional development efforts creates accountability for the staff, makes teachers more concerned about learning the standards, and emphasizes their importance.

The standards also establish a common professional development vocabulary for administrators and teachers. Administrators should ensure that central office staff members, school-level administrators, and teachers, especially those who plan adult learning experiences, have more than a cursory understanding of the standards. Distributing the standards as a handout or placing them on the front page of a strategic plan misses the mark. The value of national standards comes when everyone knows what they mean and how to use them to improve professional development. Include time to study these standards in leadership training sessions for teachers and principals. Administrators should also use the vocabulary from the standards as they work with district and school-level professional development planning teams. They can also use the standards as criteria to assess local plans and initiatives and to reject plans that clearly depart from the standards.

## Using Effective Models for Professional Development

If the goal for professional learning is to improve learning for students, then the models used to stimulate adult learning must help teachers transfer what they learn during their professional development sessions to real-life situations in their classrooms. The names Bruce Joyce and Beverly Showers are synonymous with cutting-edge research about what works in professional training. They have extensively studied the relationship between various training models and their outcomes. Joyce and Showers (2002) believe that there is enough research available on effective staff development models that school districts everywhere can have highly effective programs for adult learning that make significant changes in teaching and learning. They also assert that professional development can be effective when the training is well designed (i.e., the outcomes and components are suitably matched) and when the school climate facilitates and promotes cooperative study and practice (p. 75). They also assert that professional development can be effective for most teachers provided that the training is "well designed (i.e., the outcomes and components are suitably matched), and when the school climate facilitates and promotes cooperative study and practice" (p. 75). Figure 6.1 shows some of the key points in

FIGURE
6.1

**Training Components and Attainment of Outcomes in Terms of Percent of Participants**

| | Outcomes | | |
|---|---|---|---|
| **Components** | **Knowledge (thorough)** | **Skill (strong)** | **Tranfer (executive implementation)** |
| Study of Theory | 10 | 5 | 0 |
| Demonstrations | 30 | 20 | 0 |
| Practice | 60 | 60 | 5 |
| Peer | 95 | 95 | 95 |

Source: From *Student Achievement Through Staff Development, 3rd edition* (pg. 78) by B. Joyce & B. Showers, 2002, Alexandria, VA: ASCD

their findings. Administrators can study and use this information as a bedrock for designing effective professional training.

Research from Joyce and Showers (2002) and standards from the National Staff Development Council (2001) have significantly clarified the requirements for professional learning. We now know that lecture- or discussion-based workshops that lack demonstrations, time for processing information, and clear connections to existing practices have been empirically proven to have little effect on classroom teaching.

Should lecture-based workshops be thrown out? Should large groups of teachers and administrators cease from gathering together for professional development? If this is the only model for professional development for a school or district, these resources could be better spent on students or other school initiatives. Should teachers be organized into small teams and given time to meet regularly and develop better lessons and testing methods? The findings of Joyce and Showers (2002) on coaching, feedback, application, and practice support creating teaching teams that are focused on classroom-based improvements and common assessment.

School and district leaders are also faced with concerns about providing expertise on proven practices, improving poorly designed teaching teams, making professional development practical for classroom use and student learning, and implementing effective professional development for an entire school district. These concerns often confound school and central office leaders and teachers to such a degree that what they know about professional development effectiveness gets lost in the mire.

The effectiveness of a professional development model depends on its intended purpose and the final outcome. Mike Schmoker says, "If we are going to conduct workshops, let's insist on a radically different format" (2006, p. 111). Creating a radically different format includes considering how to use a variety of resources that will have the greatest influence on adult learning.

One of Schmoker's suggestions is to immediately link what teachers learn from a workshop to group sessions where they can develop lessons and common assessments for use in the classroom. Another idea is to pilot innovations with a single team until convincing results emerge from the work.

## Human Resources for Professional Development

Professional development models are linked to people who provide, facilitate, or generate the professional learning experience. The following list provides a description of the four types of resource people who contribute to adult learning (see also Figure 6.2 for a full listing of roles and responsibilities for each contributor):

- A **guru** (or **expert**) has the background, extensive experience, and skills to train others on a particular discipline or field of study. Many gurus are also authors who make considerable contributions to the education profession.
- **Consultants** may also be experts and authors, but in this context a consultant is a person who gains his or her knowledge by studying the experts. Consultants interpret the work of gurus in the field and transfer that understanding to teachers and other school leaders so that they can apply these practices in the classroom. A consultant also gives advice, support, and feedback.
- A **coach** or **in-district coordinator** may also be a consultant or an expert. Generally, coaches give continuous feedback to teachers and help them reflect on how to apply proven practices for school improvement. Coaches demonstrate, facilitate, and motivate teachers. There are a growing number of models for coaching (Costa & Garmston, 2002; Knight, 2004; Sweeney, 2003). Principals could act as a coach for their staff; however, it is important to distinguish between the roles of coaches and principals. Principals provide leadership for their schools; coaches help school leaders implement improvements in teaching.

- A **teacher-leader** and **members of teacher teams** facilitate their own learning. Teacher-leaders help teachers apply proven practices to real-life classroom situations. They also absorb new ideas from experts, consultants, coaches, in-house trainers, and their own investigations.

Depending on the purpose of a specific professional development session, these resource people can make substantial contributions to learning outcomes. For example, district leaders set up an overview session to assess the viability of an innovation in a particular classroom environment. Initially, the leaders decide that attending workshops or seminars conducted by a leading expert in the field seems appropriate. Realistically, these leaders must acknowledge that only 10 percent of participants walk away with a thorough knowledge on a topic based on presentations alone (Joyce & Showers, 2002).

FIGURE 6.2 **Resource People for Professional Development**

| Resource Persons | Roles and Responsibilities |
|---|---|
| **Gurus, Experts, and Authors** | • Provides keynote speeches<br>• Conducts 1- or 2-hour conference presentations<br>• Conducts half-day or full-day seminars<br>• Provides 1- or 2-day extended teaching<br>• Provides on-site visitation and teaching |
| **Consultants** | • Provides overview presentations for large groups<br>• Provides follow-up presentations for large groups<br>• Provides small-group facilitation<br>• Provides small-group presentations and discussion<br>• Performs walkthroughs with principals<br>• Provides feedback and coaching for principals and teachers<br>• Provides classroom demonstrations |
| **Coaches and District Coordinators** | • Provides continuous on-site feedback on implementation<br>• Conducts reflective conversations with teachers<br>• Oversees collaborative planning support and facilitation<br>• Facilitates individual teacher coaching cycles<br>• Provides classroom demonstrations |
| **Teacher-Leader and Teacher Teams** | • Provides classroom demonstrations<br>• Facilitates collaborative planning<br>• Conducts peer or cognitive coaching<br>• Facilitates examining student work, lesson study, collegial walkthroughs, and action research<br>• Develops common assessments |

Another example is using an experienced consultant or trainer to present theory underlying organizing and managing cooperative groups applied to a math investigation. The consultant includes demonstrations of cooperative group techniques. Then, teachers practice the techniques in their own classrooms, regroup to discuss their findings with the consultant, and prepare for the next steps. Using this model, 50–60 percent of participants could have a thorough knowledge and strong skills for this subject. In many situations, this outcome might be good, but this is not good enough for student achievement. To fully implement this strategy for all students, this model needs to include coaching and feedback for teachers. With coaching, Joyce and Showers (2002) estimate that 95 percent of participants can transfer a technique to the classroom. Note that coaching does not have to be done by a guru or a consultant (Joyce & Showers, 2002; Knight, 2004).

Coaching does not have to be done by coaches that are dedicated to a specific approach, although that model has enormous power and potential. Consider the most effective and efficient means of infusing coaching into the professional development model. Adding personnel may or may not be the solution. Omitting coaching altogether puts the effort at risk. Jim Knight at the University of Kansas Center for Research on Learning (2004) identified critical conditions for effective coaches. Readers are encouraged to explore his findings, which support the use of coaching under specific conditions. Coaching increases not only the degree to which teachers fully implement a practice but also the degree to which that implementation is true to its intended form.

Many teachers have criticized professional development models that are based on only one design option or rely too heavily on an expert to deliver the right information. Indeed, the experts provide essential ties to proven practices; however, it is the teachers' responsibility to fully implement these practices in the classroom and to work with school-based teaching teams to create their own professional learning community.

## Job-Embedded Models for Professional Development

There is a vast difference between including time in the school day for teachers to meet together and employing a gradual release of responsibility to teachers during their working hours. Teachers must have time to meet in teams and to learn and use professional development techniques that are embedded into their jobs.

Job-embedded models that improve teaching must include specific expectations and skill development for the task at hand.

Lois Brown Easton (2004) offers detailed explanations on professional development designs that have the potential for job-embedded practice. These methods include using action research, critical friends groups, lesson study, peer coaching, study groups, and a variety of protocols for examining student work. Pearson and Gallagher's gradual release of responsibility model (1983) explains how student learning progresses from dependence on a teacher for instruction to complete independence and application without teacher support. Diane Sweeney (2003) adapts the gradual release of responsibility model to adult learning and explains how certain models, particularly coaching, help teachers move from reading, observing, and watching demonstrations to using coteaching models, observations with feedback, discussions on success, and assuming leadership roles to help other teachers learn.

Regardless of the specific model selected, the means by which each method becomes a part of the school's repertoire for adult learning involves a process of obtaining more control over the innovation. Listed below are two power tools that can be used successfully with job-embedded models for professional development.

## Power Tool: The Professional Development Plan

The opening scenario from the beginning of the chapter lacks two fundamental precepts—an intense focus on professional development and full implementation of professional development methods for classroom use. Professional development workshops or sessions that are presented as the "flavor of the month" or that are offered to teachers unexpectedly by a well-known speaker need to be restructured by focusing on one proven practice at a time. School leaders need to narrow down their change initiatives, link the initiatives with a variety of professional development models, and closely monitor and evaluate how teachers implement the initiatives in their classrooms. For elementary school teachers, an intense focus on professional development includes taking on one content-area improvement at a time or implementing a single teaching practice that can be applied across the curriculum. In secondary schools, an intense focus involves encouraging teachers to study one set of proven practices or specific content-area practices that have the highest potential for improving student learning.

An intense focus on professional development requires that teachers are persistent in learning to apply a narrow set of proven practices. When a set of practices becomes embedded into teachers' routines and students demonstrate that they are benefiting from the initiatives, move on to the next innovation in the professional development plan. School administrators will know to move forward when every teacher uses the practices learned through professional development at a high level. The professional development plan provides the power tool for achieving an intense focus and full implementation that lead to improved student learning. The plan itself, like all blueprint processes, does not improve learning. School improvement comes from implementing the plan, helping teachers shape their actions around effective professional learning, and aligning all professional development efforts.

## School Professional Development Plans

The purpose of a written professional development plan is to outline the objectives and activities for adult learning. There is no absolute set of components for a professional development plan; however, we suggest the following essential questions as a guide for creating the plan:

**1. What initiatives in your school improvement plan require a focus on professional development?** Answering this question will frame a school's focus for adult learning. The school improvement plan may include more professional development needs than can reasonably be completed in a single year. Narrow the scope by focusing on one initiative.

**2. What professional development activities will you use to accomplish your goals? When will you do each activity? What will it cost?** This part of the plan describes all the events and activities that contribute to adult learning, including initiatives that cost money or involve resource people or materials. A well-constructed plan includes multiple activities that match the standards for effective professional learning. Writing this section will give school administrators a better idea of what knowledge and skills teachers will need to acquire to implement proven practices.

**3. How will you evaluate your professional development plan? Is the plan improving teaching and learning for teachers and students?** Describe the specific evaluation tools and the level of evaluation for each innovation in the professional development plan. Develop a plan that will gauge how well teachers are implementing specific professional development techniques and how the techniques are affecting student learning.

4. **What is the total budget for professional development? How will the money be spent?** Consider all the sources that are available to support adult learning activities and record the costs for each activity.

The touchstone texts at the end of the chapter provide numerous templates and forms to help school administrators shape their professional development documents. Similar to the school improvement plan, teachers and principals should collaborate to determine what adult learning is needed and how to provide it using a variety of practices that are based on quality standards for professional development.

## District Professional Development Plans

A district plan for professional development should align with the district's curriculum and instruction initiatives that are already under way. Additionally, the plan should also include activities that address mandated initiatives such as school safety, health issues, and state or federal requirements. Each school cannot reasonably address each topic and also develop an intense focus on one proven practice; therefore, the district's plan should only include essential topics that will influence the greatest number of classrooms.

With the proper perspective, school leaders look to the district plan to see what adult learning activities the district plans to provide. School leaders can then add their own school-based professional development to ensure that teachers are fully implementing proven practices in the classroom and addressing other specific topics based on the school's data. In small districts, the district plan and school plan for professional development may be the same; however, even for these districts, school leaders need to scrutinize and carefully coordinate professional development models for both elementary and secondary teachers. Figure 6.3 presents a list of red flags for district professional development planning and suggestions for supporting school-based work.

The district's written plan should include addendums that show each school's efforts and summary documents that display each school's primary professional development efforts for the upcoming year. These documents will help district leaders link schools with similar professional development needs. Leaders should distribute the summaries to principals and teacher leaders throughout the district to encourage partnerships among schools. School leaders can also use these summaries

| FIGURE 6.3 | Effective and Ineffective Plans for Professional Development |
|---|---|
| **Professional Development Plans That Don't Work** | **Professional Development Plans That Work** |
| The district professional development committee is comprised of teachers who only put a rubber stamp on decisions. | The committee looks at national standards for professional development to educate the committee on structure and functionality. |
| Central office administrators plan the district's professional development efforts with little or no input from teachers or school leaders. Teachers and school leaders are dependent on district-sponsored events for professional development, or they are surprised to learn about activities they are required to attend. | Central office administrators develop relationships with trust and respect to ensure effective collaboration. Administrators also welcome input from everyone. |
| In districts with multiple sites, professional development planning is done by a representative committee, and principals have limited involvement in or knowledge of the plan until the activities are announced. | The planning committee ensures that all principals have knowledge of the district's professional development activities as they are designed. The committee also allows principals to have input about when and how the topics fit into the overall picture for professional development. |
| The number of district-required professional development activities prevents teachers from participating in their school's professional development activities. | The planning committee monitors the number and type of professional development activities in the district's plan. The committee also limits the number of district-sponsored professional development events, sets annual priorities, and implements the activities based on the perspective of a single teacher. |
| The planning for professional development occurs with little or no regard for curriculum and instruction initiatives. | The planning committee establishes and measures all professional development efforts for the purpose of improving teaching and learning. The committee also institutes an administrative structure that directly links curriculum and instruction to professional development and assessment. |
| The district's professional development efforts consume all the available funding for professional development. School-based professional development plans are underfunded or lack sufficient resources to be fully implemented. If the school's plans consume the entire budget, this is also a red flag. | All central office administrators and principals know the national standards for professional development and are familiar with a variety of effective professional development models. The planning committee negotiates the district's and the schools' role in professional development, and they help both parties divide the funds accordingly. |

to develop a professional development plan for an individual or a group of teachers. District and school leaders should discuss and revise the district's plan if the demands from the initiatives prevent teachers from putting these plans into practice.

## Individual Professional Development Plans

Another model for professional development allows individual teachers to develop their own plan for improving their knowledge and skills. This individual approach is supported by the National Association of Secondary School Principals and was cited in their 1996 report titled *Breaking Ranks: Changing an American Institution*. Lindstrom and Speck (2004) also cite several districts where individual plans form the framework for professional learning in a district. Teacher evaluation systems such as the one proposed by Charlotte Danielson and Thomas McGreal (2000) include a professional development track for tenured teachers that may be voluntary or required. They also provide descriptions of districts where individual plans work to raise the level of teaching and learning.

Individual plans may enhance professional practice if teachers need additional knowledge and skills for effective teaching other than those targeted in the school or district professional development plans. Danielson and McGreal (2000) emphasize the importance of establishing parameters for individual plans. These parameters help teachers and administrators differentiate plans that are merely a paperwork shuffle from plans that actually transform classroom teaching. District guidelines that are established collaboratively with principals and teachers can further clarify what is acceptable for an individual professional development plan.

Aligning a school's or district's guidelines for individual professional development plans with established standards for professional learning increases the possibility of teachers incorporating best practices in the classroom.

When individual professional development plans are only loosely aligned to the school's overall plan or connected to a generic district framework, the gap between what teachers know and what they do widens. Individual plans must be connected to the school's plans. Few teachers can reasonably initiate significant changes in their work behaviors and practices without a specific focus. Over the years, we have observed individual plans for teachers that targeted good practices or techniques, but the plans were unconnected to the school's goals. As a result, these individual plans are abandoned when school-level activities and expectations gear up.

Another challenge with individual plans is that they may appear to be connected with the school's plan, but the final paperwork reveals that there were no systems in place to make teachers accountable for student learning or their own improvement. Effective individual plans include clear parameters for selecting topics, timelines, evaluation tools, and a system for accountability.

## Power Tool: Look Fors

Good professional development includes clearly defining what appropriate and effective instructional innovation looks like in the classroom. Implementing a new innovation requires that every teacher participates in the plan at a high level. An essential part of creating effective professional development is setting clear expectations. Look fors help establish standards for high-quality innovations in the classroom and bridge the gap between learning what to do and doing it.

### Definition and Purposes for Look Fors

A look for is a clear statement that describes an observable teaching or learning behavior, strategy, outcome, product, or procedure. Observers search for look fors when they visit a classroom or examine student work. Teachers can reflect on look fors to compare their teaching practices to established standards, define what they learn through professional development, and develop descriptors for classroom practice. School and district leaders can use look fors to define standards for all classrooms, identify achievable and identifiable improvements, and unify a school around a common focus and set of practices. See Figure 6.4 for an overview on developing general look fors.

### Examples of Look Fors

Generic look fors have clear descriptions or indicators on classroom design, general standards for curriculum implementation, and instructional techniques. These general standards are good starting points for teacher team discussions about good teaching practice. Specific look fors describe a detailed teaching technique or proven practice. These look fors are directly connected to specific innovations that teachers study in professional development workshops.

Nancy worked with an elementary school faculty to create a set of look fors on a writer's workshop. During the workshop, teachers studied findings from leading thinkers and authors such as Lucy Calkins (1994), Nancie Atwell (1987), Donald Graves (1983), and Ralph Fletcher and JoAnn Portalupi (2001). Teachers began to put the writing techniques into practice and experimented with components of the writer's workshop model. Although teachers were expected to implement all parts of the workshop, the principal observed some inconsistencies in the classrooms. Nancy assisted this faculty by defining the look fors from the perspective of the

| FIGURE 6.4 | **Developing General Look Fors** |
|---|---|

**Step 1**
Prepare for the activity by reading and thinking about what good teaching and learning looks like, sounds like, and feels like. Ask each individual to consider what he or she believes a great classroom includes based on prior experience as a learner. Show photos, posters, or videos of a classroom, or visit an actual classroom together to set the stage for thinking about what is required for powerful teaching and learning. Ideally, identifying look fors comes from thoughtful study of a particular aspect of teaching and learning, not just opinions without solid reasoning and evidence.

**Step 2**
Ask each participant to make a list of 8–10 descriptors of effective practice. If you were visiting a classroom, what would you look for that indicates powerful teaching and learning? What would it look like? Feel like? Sound like? How do you know what good work looks like?

**Step 3**
Combine participants into pairs or triads. Ask each group to combine their individual descriptors and identify 5–7 key descriptors or look fors that they believe to be most important.

**Step 4**
Ask members of each group to write their key descriptors on chart paper or on large cards that are then taped or hung on the wall for all to see.

**Step 5**
After each group has recorded its descriptors, read aloud each descriptor and categorize the list into subgroups that are similar. For example, you can combine all the descriptors for classroom design or room arrangement. You may need to rewrite or draw lines to show which descriptors go together. Use colored markers to circle like descriptors.

**Step 6**
Using group consensus and discussion, determine a final list of descriptors that become the look fors for the group. This final list might include 5–15 items, depending on the size of the group and its diversity of ideas.

**Step 7**
Using group consensus and discussion and the school's improvement plan and professional development plan, select 1–3 look fors that the group can agree to focus on for the year. Focusing on too many look fors at once reduces implementation.

teachers. After agreeing on what each part of the workshop would look like at their school, the whole group made a commitment to include the look fors in their workshops. This school's efforts appear in Figure 6.5. This figure shows what these teachers knew about this model, how they modified the look fors to encompass their new understanding, and how they solidified their learning with continued use of this model. Eventually the look fors from the writer's workshop helped principals promote reflection during team meetings and give feedback to teachers after visiting their classrooms.

FIGURE 6.5

## Writer's Workshop Look Fors

**Classroom Environment and Climate**

- Writing supplies available to students and easily located in the classroom
- Seating permits space for writing, conferencing, mini-lessons, sharing, and displays of work
- Procedures for each part of the workshop are taught and practiced
- Climate of risk taking
- Space for display of student work
- Resources are readily available to students (e.g., dictionaries, word walls)
- Examples of good work are modeled and discussed

**Mini-lessons**

- Clear, appropriate objectives are posted and/or stated
- Teacher models effective writing or uses student work as model
- Lessons are short, focused, and directed toward objective
- Evidence of continuity of lessons based on student need
- Topics are appropriate to the developmental level of students
- Content of mini-lessons include the writing process, writing traits, and writing genres

**Status Check**

- Teacher checks quickly with each student in regard to their writing progress
- System in place to record and monitor each child's progression
- Students self-report and evaluate where they are in their writing process
- Status checks are short (less than 1 minute) per student
- Students are aware of the purpose and procedure of the status check

**Writing Time**

- "Bubble of silence" observed during some of the writing time
- Students write
- Teacher actively conferences and monitors student writing
- Students self-assess and use peer assessment
- Topics are student-driven with a choice of topic within the genre being studied
- Prompt writing is limited but incorporated into overall writing plan
- Students use resources during writing (e.g., dictionaries, word walls, and thesauruses)
- Writing time happens every day in writer's workshop and occupies the largest block of time

**Conferencing**

- System in place to ensure that every student benefits from conferencing time
- Teacher conferences with several students each day
- Focus is on the writer, not fixing the writing
- Conferences include references to teaching points made in previous mini-lessons
- Teachers ask questions of writers and listen to responses
- Teacher sits with student and makes frequent eye contact
- Teacher uses system for recording conference information and observation

| FIGURE 6.5 | Writer's Workshop Look Fors *(continued)* |
|---|---|

**Author Share**

- A system for allowing everyone to share is in place
- Procedures for appropriate sharing and listening are taught and practiced
- Consistent time in each classroom for author sharing

**Assessment and Evaluation**

- Explanations and list of skills for a particular genre are clearly communicated to students
- Students are able to explain the elements of the scoring guide and show examples in their work
- Scoring guides are written in developmentally appropriate language
- Student work displays are linked to specific standards or scoring guide
- Teacher and students use schoolwide terminology and procedures for scoring
- Published work is kept in folders or portfolios
- Expectations are set for students regarding the amount and type of writing during grading period

**NOTE:** The faculty used a carousel process to determine these look fors. It began with charts around the room for the various components of the workshop. The large group was divided into smaller groups who worked at each station, then rotated to read what previous groups had done and added their own ideas. Reference materials such as professional texts the group had been studying were available to check specific points. After the group finalized the look fors, a ceremony was held where participants took a "pledge" to use these look fors as the framework for their writer's workshop.

Figure 6.6 contains examples of both generic and specific look fors. These examples emphasize the following:

- Look fors are powerful when they are developed by the people who use the innovation. We have learned that look fors that are created with a top-down approach are not as effective with teachers. A discussion on creating look fors with principals appears later in this chapter.
- Look fors created by teachers are best when they are flexible, because new understandings will emerge with practice and feedback.
- Long lists of look fors that are not supported by sufficient professional development will not help teachers with classroom implementation. Identify a practice and define the most essential and salient features. Next, select a few look fors to ensure that all the components of a practice become part of the descriptors. Add more details as implementation becomes complete.

## How to Develop Look Fors

Look fors should be developed as a part of the process of learning any new innovation. The following tips are essential for creating powerful look fors:

FIGURE 6.6

**Examples of Look Fors**

**Look Fors for General Teaching and Learning**

- Displays of student work show what students know and are able to do
- Daily lessons match district and state curriculum goals
- Students are actively engaged in learning
- Students are asked to justify their thinking and their responses
- Students participate in creating criteria for scoring guides and use the guides to evaluate their own work and the work of their peers
- Students are engaged in discussion and independent thought about high-level problems and questions; low-level recall is minimized
- Teachers pose questions and wait for students to think and respond; every student is accountable for an answer

**Look Fors for Proven Practices**
**Guided Reading for Primary Grades**

- Teacher supplies each student with his or her own text
- Teacher gives each student the opportunity to read independently at his or her own pace
- Teacher circulates among the group and observes each student's reading behavior
- Teacher supports each reader's attempts to solve problems
- Teacher helps readers initiate efficient problem-solving strategies

- Avoid creating look fors before conducting a professional development workshop on a new practice. Begin the work only after teachers have had focused study and reflection on the practice.
- Use a process-oriented discussion to develop the indicators.
- Use a consultant or an in-house content expert for quality control and to ensure that the main ideas are embedded in the look for list.

Joseph Werlinch and Otto Graf, consultants and professors at the University of Pittsburgh, adapted the jigsaw group process to develop look fors. This process involves using focused questions to narrow a user's thinking about an innovation (see Figure 6.7 for more detail). This technique saves considerable time for administrators and teachers because they can create look fors by using broad questions based on the fundamentals of the innovation rather than beginning with a blank page. For example, administrators and teachers can use the jigsaw technique for a writing workshop by predetermining broad categories such as mini-lessons, status check, conferencing, student writing, and sharing specific indicators. Because these broad categories are preselected, widely accepted, and understood, the shared decision-making process will not be compromised.

FIGURE 6.7 **Jigsaw Process for Look Fors**

**PREPARATION**

Design questions or tasks that relate to the goal of the activity. Put one question or task on a page. Print the pages so that each question or task is printed on different color of paper. Collate the pages into sets with one page of each color in the set.

**THE PROCESS**

**A.** Divide large group into smaller work groups of 4-6 participants, depending on the number of colored pages used.

**B.** Distribute sets of colored pages to each group so that each participant has one page. (In very large groups, two participants could share a single colored page.) Each participant is responsible for recording the ideas and input from the work group regarding the question or task on the colored page that he or she is assigned. In addition, each participant contributes to the discussion from all the other pages.

**C.** The work group discusses the question or task on each colored page. The person responsible records the group's ideas. Set a time limit for each page.

**D.** The facilitator stops the discussion and redistributes the participants according to the colors of the pages. All participants responsible for recording a particular color are grouped together. Each newly formed group consists of participants who have recorded information about their assigned question or task.

**E.** The newly formed color groups share the ideas that their former work groups developed. Ideas are collated and combined on a chart or master list to represent the collective wisdom of the group. Set a time limit per page.

**F.** Follow-up Strategies

1. Each color group prepares a chart of the collective ideas that is placed in an area where the faculty or group will see it over the coming days. Additional ideas may be added. These charts are then used to make final decisions about the course of action of the group.
2. Each color group is given a master copy page to record their ideas in the same way that they might do so on a chart. The group submits this master list to the facilitator who prepares the information and sends it out to all group members for review. For the purpose of reporting back to the large group meeting, each color group selects two of its best ideas and records them on a blank transparency. Each color group makes a brief report of its best ideas.

## Power Tool: Innovation Configurations

Gene Hall and Shirley Hord (2001) developed the Innovation Configuration (IC) after they observed a common problem among teachers—when teachers were asked to put new practices in place, they were not clear about what they were being asked to do. The IC Map provides descriptions or word pictures that illustrate the various ways that an innovation or practice can take place in a classroom. Hall and

Hord also provide users with fidelity lines that differentiate between acceptable and unacceptable implementation of a specific practice. To develop the map, they recommend developing them in groups of three to seven people. Joan Richardson (2004) and Robby Champion (2003) also describe similar processes for creating an innovation configuration map. The touchstone texts for this chapter also provide additional resources for creating an IC map. We believe that the fidelity lines and rubric-style construction for the IC maps take look fors to another level. Look fors and IC maps bridge the gap between learning about best practices and putting them to use in the classroom.

## How Do We Know If Professional Development Makes a Difference for Teaching and Learning?

Actions that are intended to improve schools, including professional development, eventually come down to one question—how will you know when you get *there?* Visioning, setting specific measurable goals for the school improvement plan, and designing look fors and innovation configurations will help administrators and school leaders define where *there* is. Getting *there* also means establishing specific evaluations to measure the effectiveness of adult learning and, ultimately, its influence on student learning. No evaluation means that teachers are not accountable for ensuring that every student benefits from the best practices available to increase achievement. Without evaluation, *there* is an illusive dream; with evaluation, schools can define where *there* is and make decisions to move to the next level or to continue persisting toward fully implementing a specific innovation or practice.

### Evaluating Professional Development

Thomas Guskey's book *Evaluating Professional Development* (2000) provides a clear, compelling, and practical guide to evaluating all aspects of professional development experiences. He warns school leaders about using evaluations that are mere documentations of what was done rather than showing proof of the effects. Guskey also cautions leaders about looking at surface features and avoiding the deepest issue of all, student learning. He outlines five critical levels for evaluating professional development. These include

- Participants' reactions (Level 1)
- Participants' learning (Level 2)

- Organization support and change (Level 3)
- Participants' use of new knowledge and skills (Level 4)
- Student learning outcomes (Level 5)

Level 1 measures how well participants liked the experience. Data from Level 1 are typically collected from a questionnaire or a survey. These data will help school leaders make decisions about providing future training and delivering adult learning experiences, but these surveys do not reveal whether or not the participants have fully implemented what they have learned in their classrooms. A high degree of satisfaction on a survey only means that participants liked the learning experience, not that they applied their learning or that students benefited from their learning. From an education consultant, a positive Level 1 evaluation only supports continued use of a particular workshop plan or consulting strategy.

Level 2 measures how much adults have learned from the professional development experience. Immediately following a workshop, facilitators can get a cursory measure at this level by asking participants to list three things they learned during the presentation. True and lasting measures at Level 2 are revealed after reflection and further study. Evaluating what adults have learned from a workshop depends on what their expectations were for a particular professional development activity. For example, if facilitators are evaluating what teachers learned from the structure of a writer's workshop, the essential elements of the structure must first be clearly defined.

In her work as an education consultant, Nancy routinely receives requests from schools to provide professional development. In her initial conversation with administrators or teachers she always asks, "What do you want to learn?" This is a Level 2 question that school leaders can use to define specific learning goals and to frame the relationship between the school and the consultant. Schools that cannot define what they want to learn have little chance of achieving lasting reforms. Level 2 information is gathered after sufficient reflection and analyzed with clear learning objectives that provide insight into what adults are learning from their professional development experience. The closer their responses are to the necessary targets for the innovation, the more beneficial the professional development session is.

Level 3 identifies any changes in the organization that support or impede how innovations are implemented. Many practices in today's schools are not geared toward progress. Teachers who are serious about changing their teaching practices need to be in environments where reasonable improvements are encouraged and promoted.

For example, implementing constructivist practices in a competitive environment where quantity is valued over quality negates the essence of this approach. A professional development experience and its accompanying innovation cannot be evaluated without examining any relevant organizational issues. Level 3 evaluations are rarely measured because politics and organizational issues often get in the way. An honest evaluation of professional development must include looking at the organizational support. Outside providers may need to be consulted for an unbiased analysis.

Level 4 measures how innovations are practiced in the classroom. At this level, it is absolutely essential to have clear and precise indicators such as look fors and innovation configurations to measure progress and to define specific behaviors and elements. Teachers who are using an innovation in the classroom should be involved in defining how it is practiced and determining quality control measures. Level 4 evaluations require ongoing measurement and an onsite or videotaped observation of the innovation that will be measured. The walkthrough (see Chapter 7) is also a valuable tool for Level 4 evaluation. Central office supervisors must insist that schools have Level 4 evaluations. The effectiveness of professional development depends on how it is applied in the classroom. All the great professional development planning, templates, and forms in the world cannot substitute for practicing an innovation. Without applying what is learned, there is no hope of improving student learning.

One final issue for level 4 is how closely teachers adhere to the innovation model. Does it really matter if a teacher implements a practice in the way it was intended? Will the applications be just as effective? Jim Knight (2004) studied classrooms with close adherence and loose adherence to the innovation model. Students showed improvement in classrooms when teachers' practices were aligned with the intended model. Level 4 evaluations provide critical data on how innovations are implemented in the classrooms, which can translate to higher student achievement.

Measurements at Level 5 reveal and clarify the purpose for the adult learning process. Precise measurements at this level help administrators and teachers answer the following questions: "Does this innovation improve student learning?" "How is this innovation influencing students?" "What do we know or still need to know?" "What evidence do we still need?" "What do the data suggest about improving our daily teaching practices?" If students don't benefit from the time, effort, and resources put into an innovation, the goal falls short of improving student achievement.

Evaluations at Level 5 match student learning measures with a practice or an innovation. When creating Level 5 evaluations, administrators and teachers should be cautious of relying solely on broad student achievement data, such as statewide assessments or national tests, to measure a specific teaching practice. These measures should not be used unless the assessment allows for sufficient disaggregation of the data to pinpoint the practice. If administrators and teachers only use broad scores for evaluation, they may think that a practice or method isn't working. In today's climate of high-stakes testing, it is tempting to evaluate professional development based on broad test scores; however, administrators and teachers must account for other factors that influence student achievement and develop other student learning indicators to accurately measure professional development methods.

Administrators and teachers should also avoid using narrow measures that miss the big picture for student achievement. For example, if a group of students were only tested on a small set of skills for reading comprehension, it would be far-fetched to claim that these data improve all reading comprehension strategies.

Level 5 evaluations should include multiple measures for student achievement. Data from these evaluations will determine the need for more emphasis on a particular practice or curricular area.

Evaluating professional development plans helps to keep administrators and teachers accountable for the school, district, or individual plans. Without an evaluation component, administrators won't know the true value of the professional development session. Millions of dollars have been spent on professional training that shows no proof of better teaching and learning. Evaluations should be a prominent component in the professional development plan. Administrators should have discussions about evaluations both during the preplanning stages for an innovation and during implementation.

## What Is the Role of District and School Leaders in Professional Development?

School and district leaders who embrace high standards for learning should be in charge of creating effective professional development and combining it with topics that are worthwhile and have merit for the organization. Thomas Guskey (2000) makes a distinction between topics that have merit and worth. Worth connects to the core mission of the district or school and answers questions such as "Is this professional development worthy of our mission and values?" and "What are the benefits of fully implementing this innovation, and how does this further our mission and vision?" A program or practice may be quite effective but not worthy of the vision. For example, the worth of a parent involvement program to increase parent contacts with the school is questionable if the school already has strong parental support and involvement.

Merit, on the other hand, has to do with the professional influence a program or practice has on the intended target. For example, adding a particular schedule or structure that appears to match the school's vision for professional development may be worth the effort, but unless the practice actually results in improvement, its merit is uncertain. Programs with merit are particularly important because without them, only superficial changes take place and needed improvements fade quickly. Schools and districts have pressures from both inside and outside of the community to put the latest and greatest programs and practices in place based on their public relations value, without any regard to their merit or potential to raise student achievement. However, as school leaders consider commercially produced programs, even those with sophisticated marketing, merit should be the standard for decision making. An essential role for central office and school leaders is to weigh the worth and merit of professional learning experiences along with other specific responsibilities and tasks.

## The Role of the Principal

The best professional development plan in the world has little chance of full implementation without the active involvement of school principals. Their responsibilities include sharing planning and implementation, modeling practices as the lead learner, facilitating structures that permit a variety of professional development models, and supervising teachers to ensure full implementation of the professional development focus.

It is possible for teachers to learn without or in spite of the principal, but full implementation of serious school reforms takes place when teachers work side by side with principals who value professional development as the means for improving learning. The principal's chief role is to align school improvement with the professional learning plan. Sharing the decision-making process unites teachers and principals and helps them to move toward the same goal. Efforts must also be made to inform and involve both teachers and principals in the design phase.

Once a great plan is in place, the principal must take the role of lead learner and attend the same professional training as teachers, even if the principal has sufficient prior knowledge of the topic. Assuming the role of lead learner is especially important for whole-faculty initiatives. These types of initiatives require principals to have a high level of understanding for full implementation to take place. When a faculty launches a major professional development effort, the principal becomes the lead learner by sitting in the front row, asking the hard questions, studying the materials, and participating in the activities. Leading the learning and dominating the learning are not the same behavior. Therefore, principals should be conscientious about not overshadowing teachers during the learning process. Another important role for principals as the lead learners is modeling the practical aspects of professional learning by managing study time and applying new understandings. Principals can model these behaviors by being active participants in team meetings and encouraging teachers to talk about teaching and learning practices.

Principals who support professional development strive to create structures that infuse a variety of professional development models into the school plan. For example, carving out time for teachers to have meetings during the school day requires principals to be tough and firm about scheduling. Other structural challenges for principals include creating plans for releasing teachers for small-group work with a visiting consultant or in-house trainer and finding funding to send teachers to a conference or workshop to gather information about a specific topic. The role of the principal is to vigilantly search for ways to further the agenda of professional learning with a variety of ways for teachers to learn.

The toughest role, by far, for a principal is supervising teachers' teaching and learning methods. Note that there is a distinction between supervising personnel and supervising curriculum and instruction. Many principals learned during their graduate school coursework that most of their supervisory activities would be focused on personnel; however, supervision also includes consistently monitoring the district curriculum and instructional strategies that will improve student learning. Principals check on the progress of the professional development plan by monitoring learning sessions with teachers, collecting data about participants' reactions and learning, and sharing the data with teachers to constantly improve adult learning experiences. Principals also visit classrooms to observe if teachers are incorporating central themes from the professional training into their classrooms. Figure 6.8 offers an observation tool for principals to use during their classroom visits as they collect data about how teachers are implementing new practices.

Working with teachers to set timelines for including new understandings into daily practice is also a critical component for principals. For example, a faculty who

**FIGURE 6.8 Observation Guide for Levels of Implementation**

| Level of Implementation | Description | Observed? |
|---|---|---|
| **No Usage** | • The teacher doesn't use the practice or use of the practice is barely observable | |
| **Level 1** | • The teacher uses an exact replica of a lesson or strategy without regard for context<br>• The teacher can only imitate from another lesson | |
| **Level 2** | • The teacher transfers the exact activity to another situation in a superficial way<br>• The teacher makes little use of complex strategies that are associated with the practice | |
| **Level 3** | • The teacher uses a practice without improving impact on students<br>• The teacher uses a practice without knowing why | |
| **Level 4** | • The teacher's use of the practice is refined<br>• The teacher seeks to coordinate his or her use of the practice with other teachers to enhance performance | |
| **Level 5** | • The teacher has a thorough knowledge of theory and practical applications for the practice<br>• The teacher knows how to make improvements and adjustments to the practice | |

completes a series of workshops on inquiry-based science instruction can work with their principal to decide on a timeline for teaching science lessons with the techniques learned. Once the timeline is determined, the principal spends observational time in classrooms looking for evidence of the teaching practices and gives teachers immediate feedback to nudge them forward or to reward their efforts. Principals should support teachers who resist implementing a specific practice or show signs of uncertainty. The principal's job is to ensure that the money and efforts devoted to professional development pay off with better teaching methods for teachers and more learning for students.

## The Role of the Central Office

Leaders from the central office make significant contributions to effective professional development. Four specific roles that central office leaders take on include structuring central office responsibilities to support professional development, maintaining an intense focus on professional development, brokering professional development options and planning sessions for schools, and building principals' capacity to plan and implement high-quality professional development.

In small districts, the central office administrator handles supervising professional development; in large districts, one or more persons are solely responsible for professional development efforts. Regardless of the size of the district, the responsibilities for administering professional development should be well structured. As previously stated in Chapter 1, we strongly believe that the central office leader who directly supervises principals must also have significant responsibility for curriculum, instruction, assessment, and professional development. Central office leaders should actively integrate and align every piece of school improvement.

Central office leaders must also be gatekeepers to maintain an intense focus on professional development. As leaders work with an intense focus, they may have an overwhelming desire to do more and to correct every deficit. However, if leaders give into this desire, they will have a group of teachers and principals who know how to put good practices in place but are too burned out to use them. When central office leaders attempt to work on all fronts, keep every initiative operating at top capacity, and institute complex improvements in teaching and learning, they are setting up a formula for defeat and exhaustion. Central office leaders must set reasonable limits on the number and type of professional development initiatives for the district and schools, regardless of political pressures to do otherwise. Leaders should start by clearly and persistently articulating what the intense focus will be in short, easily articulated terms, and they should remove any distracters that will take away from the overall goals. Central office leaders must be diligent about saying no to programs, people, and ideas that will not further the intense focus of the district and will prevent their success with school improvement.

Central office leaders should also broker partnerships between schools that have the same professional development focus. These types of partnerships will create a more collaborative climate for professional learning in a district. When central office leaders provide practices and standards for high-quality professional development to principals, school leaders can make good use of gurus, consultants, in-house staff developers, and instructional coaches as they design their own professional training. Cheri Patterson, associate superintendent of the St. Joseph School District in St. Joseph, Missouri, produces an annual booklet of professional development possibilities for schools. The brochure helps school leaders narrow down an intense focus for professional development and reduces the long hours they would need to spend locating a consultant or viewing a video study program. As principals and school leaders become more experienced in designing their own powerful professional development sessions and workshops, less hand-holding is needed from the central office. However, even veteran school leaders who are experts at preparing professional development will appreciate central office administrators like Cheri who make professional development planning more efficient and focused.

The most powerful role for central office leaders is developing capacity among school leaders. As principals develop their professional development initiatives, central office leaders become teachers and show them how to

- Identify standards for effective professional development
- Identify components of a school professional development plan
- Create strategies for including staff members in planning, implementing, and evaluating professional development
- Evaluate professional development programs and strategies
- Discuss practical ways to gather evaluation data
- Explore a variety of professional development designs and formats
- Effectively use gurus, consultants, in-house trainers, and coaches

As central office leaders build principals' capacity for professional development, they must also model good professional development standards in principal meetings and training events and hold principals accountable for what they learn in their professional development sessions. Leaders should also monitor each school's improvement and professional development plan and develop an evaluation process. The data consultation (see Chapter 4) is a good power tool for these processes. These data will help central office leaders and principals have natural discussions about what the school needs and what kind of professional development is required to build capacity.

## Reflections from the Field

"I wish principals understood that it takes more than one year to get it."
"If you can remind people of the expectations over a period of time, they will remember and utilize them."
"A little dab won't do ya when it comes to putting our professional development in place in the classroom."

These words of wisdom are direct quotes from high school and elementary staff members. These thoughts reflect a shift in teachers' thinking about what is most important to consider when revising school improvement and professional development plans for the future. It is heartwarming to hear that teachers want to use more of what they are learning and have more time for professional development, even if they express their desires through frustration. Hallelujah! What a breakthrough! Now the stage is set for implementation. When the *need to know* how to implement an effective practice emerges, implementation surges.

The question is how can principals capitalize on a faculty's self-identified *need to know*? They can start by ensuring that the action steps for the school improvement and professional development plans for the coming year remain relatively close to the current action steps. Drastic changes or a shift from one strategy to another without full implementation is what teachers fear most. This may be why some faculty members don't hurry toward implementation. They know that if they wait, a new strategy will emerge. Another way to build on teacher motivation to learn is to plan professional development for the coming year as an extension of the initiatives that are already in place. Go deeper, implement stronger, and get close to the finish line. Stay focused and you'll see the benefits.

—Nancy Mooney

## Touchstone Texts

Easton, L. (2004). *Powerful designs for professional learning*. Oxford, OH: National Staff Development Council.

Guskey, T. (2000). *Evaluating professional development*. Thousand Oaks, CA: Corwin Press.

Heck, S., Stiegelbauer, S., Hall, G., & Loucks, S. (1999). *Measuring innovation configurations: Procedures and applications*. Reprinted and distributed by Southwest Educational Development Laboratory (SEDL).

Hord, S., & Roy, P. (2003). *Moving the NSDC standards into practice: Innovation configurations*. Oxford, OH: National Staff Development Council.

Joyce, B., & Showers, B. (2002). *Student achievement through staff development. (3rd ed.)*. Alexandria, VA: ASCD.

NSDC. (2001). *National Staff Development Council standards for staff development (Rev. ed.)*. Oxford, OH: NSDC.

# 7

# Supervising Teaching, Learning, and People

Feedback is the breakfast of champions.

—*Ken Blanchard*

Supervision classes in graduate school typically focus on supervising personnel; completing necessary forms and functions for evaluations; observing, recording, and giving feedback; and developing and using criteria for teacher evaluation. While all of these functions are important for supervising personnel, supervision for teaching and learning is quite another thing. The two can and, we contend, should be connected together to develop a seamless improvement process. This chapter explains how we envision a new level of understanding and practice about supervision of teaching, learning, and people. The walkthrough and the postobservation conference are the power tools that make the work happen.

## The Pittsburgh Epiphany

In a warm, crowded classroom at the University of Pittsburgh, a group of school administrators gathered in June 1995 for the first annual meeting of the National Principal Initiative. Nancy attended the meeting with a team of senior administrators and several principals from her district. One afternoon session featured Tony Alvarado, superintendent of District 2 in New York City, and Lauren Resnick, director of the Learning Research and Development Center at the University of Pittsburgh. Alvarado passionately described how he monitored teaching and learning in a school district that was once reputed to be New York's worst but is now touted as a shining star of achievement. He talked about visiting classrooms, talking to students, and looking at student work. Alvarado linked his visits with teacher accountability for implementing massive professional development efforts to raise achievement in literacy. He promoted the central office administrator in his district to the instructional supervisor of teaching, learning, and people.

Resnick followed Alvarado with a deep talk about the principles of learning. She explained how these research-based strategies help students to learn and grow for a lifetime, not just for the next test. Resnick also described how she used "learning walks" to analyze student work, evaluate how students are thinking, and discover what they are learning.

Nancy was mesmerized by the intensity of the presentations and by the connections that she made from what she heard from these respected professionals to her own experiences as a principal and as a central office supervisor for principals. She knew from her experiences over the years that her classroom visits were the touchstone for knowing how to lead improvement in teaching and learning. Now she had a framework for aligning those visits with other aspects of school improvement. Right there in that Pittsburgh classroom, Nancy made the leap to linking accountability with supervision. Her leadership was never the same after that day.

Soon after that powerful meeting, Joe Werlinich and Otto Graf, professors at the University of Pittsburgh and leaders of the Western Pennsylvania Principal Academy, came to St. Joseph, Missouri as onsite consultants for the administration. During their visits, Nancy learned practical strategies for conducting walkthroughs and debriefing classroom visits with principals and teachers. She also discovered how to use principals' professional learning as a catalyst for building leadership capacity. Best of all, she gained confidence to go to the next level with her own supervision of teaching and learning. The lessons that she learned from those experiences are included in this chapter, along with insights and reflections for aligning the blueprint processes, supervising teaching and learning, and developing diagnostic and accountability dimensions for education reform. Without all these pieces, the overall effect of all the other work would be greatly diminished.

## From Impressions to Reality

Ann had been in her role in the central office for four years. During that time, she had focused her efforts on developing the district curriculum to improve test scores. She created a thorough process for curriculum review, development, and implementation. She monitored implementation by talking with principals, surveying teachers, and analyzing test data. Despite hours of painstaking work, gains in test scores were minor and implementation seemed fragmented at best.

Next, Ann decided to focus on school improvement plans. She developed a new template for school improvement, and she discussed the important components with principals during regularly scheduled meetings. Principals throughout the district shared their improvement plans with each other, and a team from the central office went out twice a year to encourage building staff members to discuss their plans. Even then, there were only minor improvements in test scores. It wasn't until Ann heard Nancy speak about her experiences using the walkthrough that she realized what was missing.

Although the processes that Ann used prior to incorporating the walkthroughs were necessary, they weren't enough to get the job done. Without a tool to help her monitor how principals and teachers were implementing curriculum and instruction, Ann was guided only by her own knowledge. With the walkthrough, Ann had insights into the curriculum and the data plus actual evidence from students in classrooms. The walkthroughs transformed the way Ann worked. The insights she gained from walking through classrooms throughout the district gave her a much needed context for teaching and learning initiatives. Ann's supervision was no longer based on impressions and instincts; it was now based on actual practice.

## Essential Questions

- How does supervision of teaching, learning, and people fit in a framework for school improvement?
- What are the purposes and procedures for using walkthroughs?
- How do walkthroughs aid alignment?
- How does differentiated supervision align with the blueprint processes?

Principals devote a lot of their energy and supervisory time to evaluating personnel. They complain that their time for supervision is dominated by completing system requirements, but they admit that the system itself does little to raise student achievement or increase the mission of teaching as a profession. Well-intentioned and enlightened principals crave to be in the classroom with an eye on learning and time to be a coach, colleague, and encourager for teachers. How can these seemingly opposing processes be part of the same school improvement framework? Sergiovanni (1992, 2007), Hunter (1986), Glanz and Sullivan (2000), and Blasé and Blasé (1997) give us enormous background and insights into supervision, including structuring conversations with teachers, competencies associated with supervision, and moral implications. This chapter does not presume to supersede their thinking or research. We offer two practical power tools, the walkthrough and the postobservation conference, to help principals link supervision for teaching, learning, and people. Both tools can be tied directly to the school improvement and professional development plans. The tools also include specific formative feedback and reflection with teachers.

In recent years, the walkthrough has emerged as a topic in professional literature and professional development sessions for administrators (Downey et al., 2004; Ginsberg & Murphy, 2002; Richardson, 2001). There are several models for conducting walkthroughs, such as the three-minute walkthrough (Downey et al., 2004) and the classroom walkthrough (Ginsberg, 2004). We applaud using walkthroughs as a way to enhance instructional leadership. The precise formats, forms, and procedures for walkthroughs are not as important as getting principals and central office administrators into classrooms to focus on teaching practices and student learning. It is also critical for leaders to provide feedback to teachers that is linked to the school improvement and professional development plan. We share the procedures that we believe work well, and we caution leaders against adopting an attitude that one model is the one right way for conducting a walkthrough. The walkthrough is one of the most powerful tools in the supervision arsenal, and it is the tool that aligns all the other blueprint processes.

## Creating a Climate for Supervision

Creating a climate of trust and respect helps to foster alignment for the blueprint processes. Developing an atmosphere where teachers can create quality displays of student work is also a critical component for lining up school improvement efforts.

### Building a Climate of Trust and Respect

Fundamental to all the work of school improvement is the underlying climate in which reform takes place. Leaders need to know what inspires people to step out their comfort zones, make long-term changes in their teaching practices, and embrace reflection, dialogue, and self-assessment for improvement. Creating trusting relationships with supervisors and colleagues is a top priority. Robert Evans

(1996) notes, "We admire leaders who are honest, fair, competent, and forward-looking. Although these qualities seem so obvious that they are easy to gloss over, they are the basis of trust." Jo and Joseph Blasé (1997) studied the practices of effective principals from the teachers' perspective. They say, "Prevalent negative associations that derive from 'control supervision' must give way to various forms of collegiality among educators.... Supervision should work toward the development of professional *dialogue* among educators."

What should a leader do to develop trust and respect? Thomas Sergiovanni (2000) refers to authentic leadership practices to describe the ideal climate for improvement. He says, "Authentic leaders anchor their practice in ideas, values, and commitments; exhibit distinctive equalities of style and substance; and can be trusted to be morally diligent in advancing the enterprises they lead. Authentic leaders, in other words, display character, and character is the defining characteristic of authentic leadership." Richard Wallace and colleagues (1997) list the following character traits as ideal qualities for school leaders: fosters trust and respect, is open to innovation, encourages teacher empowerment, shares norms and values, creates time to meet and discuss, uses and makes time for reflective dialogue, encourages a collective focus on student learning, and has a cognitive skill base. Principals and central office administrators who want school improvement that lasts must identify their own core values and beliefs. Trust and respect grow in a climate where leaders lead from their own high moral ground and good character. All the school improvement processes in the world cannot cover up for serious character flaws. Ultimately, the level of trust and respect that followers have for their leaders determines their success. Reflecting on the importance of building trust and respect, identifying core values and beliefs, and acting within a framework of honesty and integrity are necessary steps for effective supervision.

## Displaying Student Work

On a practical level, building a climate for strong instructional supervision also includes taking the opportunity to view student work. Observers must begin to shift the purpose of their classroom visits from focusing on the teacher to looking at student work. As observers begin viewing student work, they should evaluate the work based on the rigor of the content, the process for the assignment, and students' thinking level and understanding. Displaying student work uncloaks teachers' goals and clarifies what is taking place in the classroom; however, revealing students' work often creates anxiety for many teachers.

When Nancy first explored the notion of using student displays as more than decorations or hallway showcases, she knew that she needed to show what effective displays looked like and define their purpose. Principal Jeaneen Boyer developed specific look fors (see Figure 7.1 for more information) that added clarity to the expectations for displays. There were still teachers who didn't understand the purpose of displaying work, even though they could create much better displays.

As principals work with teachers to teach them how to effectively use student displays for monitoring teaching and learning, they have to begin a dialogue with teachers about the intent and purpose for the displays. Principals can use these conversations to establish guidelines and timelines for displaying work in hallways and classrooms. They also need to take this time to emphasize the importance of displaying student work that shows the content of the curriculum and students' thinking processes, self-assessment, and comprehension. Principals should ensure that teachers aren't just displaying work that is pretty or decorative. Principals can also show photographs or invite teachers to visit other schools to see what effective student displays can look like and accomplish. Finally, they should state how they will use the displays as part of their walkthrough feedback.

## Purposes for Displaying Student Work

Student displays serve a variety of purposes for classroom teachers, including:

- **Analyzing quality student work.** By looking at displays of good work, observers, teachers, and students can see what is valuable about an assignment and how it was assessed. Viewing good work helps teachers and students generate ideas for improvement.
- **Showcasing students' efforts.** Displaying students' learning efforts emphasizes the importance of this part of the learning process. Showcasing efforts may mean displaying work that is not perfect; therefore, teachers need to clearly indicate what parts of the work are worthy of showcasing and why.
- **Communicating classroom efforts with adults.** Schools that include student displays throughout the building show adults what is happening in the classroom. Few methods convey more information about student progress than having considerable amounts of student work on display for adults to view, enjoy, and ponder.

**FIGURE 7.1** **Observation Guide for Displays of Student Work**

| Subjects Displayed | Observations |
|---|---|
| Reading | |
| Writing | |
| Math | |
| Social Studies | |
| Science | |
| **Presentation of Display** | |
| Neat? | |
| Organized? | |
| Easily viewed by adults and students? | |
| Changed monthly? | |
| Easily understood by guests and other classroom teachers? | |
| **Displayed Assignment or Subject** | |
| Includes an explanation of the assignment? | |
| Shows a clearly labeled purpose or objective? | |
| Includes small sampling of class? | |
| Shows high grade-level expectations? | |
| Includes labels as needed? | |
| **Displayed Scoring Guide or Evaluation** | |
| Specifically states areas for student assessment? | |
| Emphasizes content, process, or both? | |
| Tool presented in grade-level language? | |
| Easily understood and used by students? | |
| Includes a clarifying statement if the tool is not used due to class project or teaching and modeling? | |
| **Application and Knowledge Demonstrated in Display/ Display Correlation with District Curriculum** | |
| Shows progression of skills as applicable? | |
| Showcases class, group, or individual projects or process? | |
| Shows appropriate grade-level material? | |
| Display showcases material related to SOS? | |
| Display matches district curriculum? | |
| **Rigor and High-Level Thinking in Display** | |
| High standards are expected and adhered to in classroom work? | |
| Deep thinking about the content is encouraged even if the content isn't difficult? | |
| Students are engaged in actively applying their knowledge? | |
| Display shows everyday rigor and high-level thinking? | |
| Display has real-life application? | |
| **TOTAL SCORE** | |

Source: Adapted from *Displays of Student Work Scoring Guide,* by J. Boyer, 2006, St. Joseph, MO. Adapted with permission.

- **Monitoring teaching and learning.** Principals and other school administrators can evaluate and gauge the effectiveness of curriculum goals and process standards by viewing displays of student work. Because these displays reveal authentic learning from the classroom, leaders can use this work to give teachers feedback and encouragement.

### Guidelines for Displaying Student Work

Presentations for student displays should be neat, organized, easily viewed by adults and students, changed monthly, and easily understood by other classroom teachers and building guests. Good displays include an explanation of the assignment, the purpose or objective, a sampling of students from the class, and high grade-level expectations. Principals can also view more guidelines in Figure 7.1 and a question and answer handout for student displays in Appendix E (see p. 181). In addition to the guidelines for good student displays, listed below are examples of displays to avoid when showcasing student work:

- Workbook pages with perfect or near-perfect answers and no context or explanation
- Student writing in adult language with identical text
- Student work with no explanation, scoring guide, clear purpose, or context
- Spelling and math tests that include 100 percent scores with no comments or context
- Student displays that only show star-quality artwork or award-winning essays or science projects
- Student displays that are posted too high for other students to see
- Identical art projects with no context or explanation
- Bare walls with little or no student work

## Conducting Walkthroughs

The walkthrough is an organized classroom visit that central office administrators and principals use to observe teaching and learning. The walkthrough keeps teachers accountable for implementing the school improvement plan and helps to determine if the staff is on target for the professional development plan. The walkthrough is also a power tool that principals can use to assess the level of teaching and learning in the building. Leaders and colleagues can use a variety of methods such as the principal (or solo), collegial, supervisory, and event walkthroughs for different purposes. The mainstay of the walkthrough process is the principal walk-through.

Inevitably, when we are discussing the walkthrough with principals, many of them share that they have been walking through the building for years. It is rare to find a graduate course on the principalship that doesn't emphasize the importance of high visibility throughout the school as a factor for effective leadership. Thus, it is extremely important for us to distinguish the difference between the *walkthrough* and *walking around*. Both are important processes; however, they have distinct purposes, procedures, and results.

We define walking around as the process of principals making their rounds throughout the school. Depending on the size of the building, the principal can complete a walk around in 20–30 minutes. Typically, a principal will walk around the hallways, peek in classrooms, and greet students and teachers during high visibility times such as when students enter school in the morning, change classes, or prepare for dismissal. Walking around serves many purposes for the principal. First, it provides the principal with a presence throughout the school and communicates to staff and students that they are important. Second, it helps principals to develop relationships with students. When principals meet and greet students in the hallways by using their names, it makes students feel like they are an important part of the school. Finally, walking around helps the principal get a pulse for the school climate. The differences between the walkthrough and walking around are summarized in Figure 7.2.

## The Walkthrough Process

The four fundamentals of the walkthrough are focusing, walking, reflection, and feedback. The first step in the walkthrough process is to establish a focus for observation in the classrooms. Establishing a focus allows the principal to concentrate on specific behaviors that enhance the quality of their feedback. Developing a set of look fors is an important step in this process. (Refer to Chapter 6 for more information on look fors.) For example, principals can narrow their focus by looking in classrooms to find examples of student work that show how students are putting their knowledge and skill to use in practical ways. In one classroom, this might mean examining student work to see how students learn and apply the process of

| FIGURE 7.2 | Walkthrough Versus Walking Around | |
|---|---|---|
| | **Walkthrough** | **Walking Around** |
| **Purpose** | • Teachers are held accountable for implementing the school improvement and professional development plans<br>• Principals can assess the level of teaching and learning | • Principals are generally visible throughout the school<br>• Principals get to know students<br>• Principals can see the big picture for the school |
| **Process** | • Principals can identify specific look fors and schedule a large block of time to observe classrooms, talk to students, and examine student work to gauge the level of implementation | • Principals briefly step in and out of classrooms, walk around hallways, and capture a quick look at what is happening throughout the school |
| **Frequency** | • Principals perform walkthroughs once a week in all classrooms in the school | • Principals walk around on a daily basis |
| **Duration** | • Principals will spend 3–5 minutes in each classroom<br>• Total time varies | • Principals will spend a total of 20–25 minutes stepping in and out of classrooms and walking the halls |
| **Feedback** | • Principals will provide formal and informal methods to validate teaching practices that match the look fors | • No formal methods |

writing a research report. Although the activities change from classroom to classroom, the primary focus remains the same. During the walkthrough, the principal looks for active use of knowledge that is built into practical applications. Ideally, the focus is tied directly to the school's professional development and school improvement plans and answers the question "What will you be looking for today?"

The second step in a walkthrough is to walk in and out of classrooms for the purpose of observing what students are learning. While it is not necessary or even possible to see every classroom, visiting even one classroom every day gets the process going and sustains the focus on teaching and learning. The walk may include examining student work posted inside or outside the classroom, interviewing students, looking at student projects or work folders, and observing the learning as it happens. The main thing is to walk through classrooms with an eye on teaching and learning.

The third step in the walkthrough is reflection. A walkthrough without reflection is walking around. As mentioned earlier in the chapter, there are benefits to walking around; however, in order to improve teaching and learning, principals and other observers need to devote some time to reflect on what they observed. Reflection may be as simple as making mental notes about follow-up strategies. It also includes purposeful planning for feedback and some form of documentation.

The final step for the walkthrough is feedback. Feedback is the breakfast of champions! Even world-class athletes seek feedback and hire coaches to help them see what they cannot see themselves. An essential part of walkthroughs is giving feedback to staff members. Letters, memos, notes, informal conversations, group debriefings, and e-mail messages can be combined to communicate the lessons learned from walking through classrooms and reflecting on student work. There are a variety of strategies for giving feedback to match the various purposes for walkthroughs. Walkthrough feedback needs to validate the teaching and learning practices that are specified in the look fors. Some general tips for feedback include:

- **Validate good practice.** Validate examples of good practice. Keep in mind that setting clear expectations for continuing a behavior or practice starts with identification. By validating good practice, principals and other observers raise teachers' awareness of the practice and elevate the practice to a level where the teacher can continue implementation. Go beyond telling teachers that they have done a good job, and identify specific practices that work. For this type of feedback, remember to validate good practices, not close approximations.
- **Notice close approximations.** Note when teachers attempt to implement close approximations of strategies and techniques learned through professional development. This type of feedback is powerful and helps to push the school's professional development goals forward faster. Comment and compliment the teacher on attempting to use a new strategy, program, or practice.
- **Encourage reflection.** Principals and other observers can foster reflection about techniques and practices by asking participants to share any observations that they are still wondering about. They can nudge participants by posing phrases such as "I'm wondering about ..." or "I'd be interested in knowing..."

Figure 7.3 provides some specific examples of feedback that could be used to validate, notice approximations, and encourage reflection.

## Conducting Staff Orientations for Walkthroughs

Before principals begin conducting regular walkthroughs, it is important to give the faculty an orientation on the purpose and intent. Each faculty has its own

**FIGURE 7.3 Examples of Walkthrough Feedback**

| Feedback | Sounds Like... |
|---|---|
| **Validating Good Practice** | "Your use of a sponge activity to start the class period increased student participation right away."<br><br>"Great use of a graphic organizer to help students comprehend the major concepts in the chapter! I could see the lights going on for students." |
| **Noticing Approximations** | "When your students work in groups, the level of engagement increases. Keep experimenting with ways to ease the transitions between whole-group and small-group activities. You and your students are making great progress. Bravo!" |
| **Encouraging Reflection** | "I'm wondering about how much the students are remembering about the vocabulary introduced in class. What other ways can the vocabulary be presented?"<br><br>"I'd be interested in knowing more about the assessments you are using for the project you assigned. How will students know what good work looks like before the assignment is completed?" |

culture; therefore, there is no one right way to accomplish this task. There are, however, some wrong ways to begin this process. Some practices to avoid include:

- **Neglecting to clearly inform the faculty of the intent and purpose of the walkthroughs before they begin.** Principals and other administrators should clarify these points in various forums, including faculty meetings, principal memos, leadership team discussions, and informal conversations.
- **Giving feedback after a walkthrough that sounds like an accusation or a condemnation.** Feedback needs to be validation that reinforces effective teaching and learning. If critical feedback is necessary, move into a clinical supervision mode. Keep walkthroughs positive.
- **Conducting walkthroughs without giving feedback.** Faculty members want to know what the observers are seeing. Feedback helps to build trust.

There are a variety of ways to involve faculty members in walkthroughs and clarify their concerns, including the following:

- **Holding the orientation session in a classroom.** Use the environment to point out positive aspects of teaching and learning, such as room design, displays of work, or student work samples. Pick a classroom where it is easy to validate good practices. The leader for the orientation session could casually say, "If you were doing a walkthrough in this classroom, what do you see that tells you that effective teaching and learning are taking place?"

- **Organizing whole-faculty walkthroughs in classrooms when students are not in session.** Give teachers a short list of look fors that can be seen without the need to talk to students. Go in and out of classrooms looking for things on the list. Establish a ground rule that only validating comments can be made. Practice together and debrief.
- **Taking faculty members on a daily walkthrough.** This works especially well at the secondary level with department chairs or teams. Visit several classrooms and encourage teachers to reflect on what they see that supports good teaching practices. The word will spread that walkthroughs are about finding and validating things that work.

## Power Tool: The Supervisory Walkthrough

The supervisory walkthrough is an opportunity for the principal and the central office administrator in charge of teaching and learning to walk through the school together to monitor school improvement efforts. The supervisory walkthrough provides an opportunity for the central office administrator to mentor and guide principals. The purpose of the supervisory walkthrough is to raise the bar for accountability for implementing school improvement initiatives. This process provides concrete help for principals regarding teaching and learning at their school. The supervisory walkthrough helps to develop and maintain a relationship of trust and respect between the principal and central office administrator. The supervisory walkthrough is similar to the principal walkthrough. The steps include planning and prebriefing, walking, debriefing, and following up with feedback. Figure 7.4 compares the roles and responsibilities for both leaders during the supervisory walkthrough.

Prior to the central office administrator's visit to the building, the principal needs to announce the time and date of the visit. This supervisory walkthrough usually takes two to three hours. In most instances, we recommend that the supervisory walkthrough be a planned visit. It would be unfair to drop in and expect a large chunk of time from a busy principal. An unexpected visit does little to build a trusting relationship between administrators. The purpose of the visit is to monitor school improvement efforts and to mentor the principal. The supervisory

FIGURE 7.4 **Roles and Responsibilities of Administrators During the Supervisory Walkthrough**

| | Central Office Administrator | Building Principal |
|---|---|---|
| **Roles** | • Mentors principal<br>• Identifies and validates practices that align with the school's improvement efforts<br>• Outlines plans and ideas that aid in continuous improvement | • Identifies look fors for observation<br>• Shares strengths and concerns regarding teaching and learning practices in the school<br>• Listens, asks questions, takes notes regarding observations and pre- and post-conversations |
| **Responsibilities** | • Schedules walkthrough<br>• Facilitates discussion before and after walkthrough<br>• Ties teaching and learning practices to school improvement and professional development plans<br>• Provides feedback to school administrators | • Notifies staff members<br>• Provides copies of school improvement and professional development plans<br>• Provides feedback to building staff |

walkthrough provides an opportunity to have an honest and in-depth conversation about the school's teaching and learning practices. This open candor cannot happen if principals feel like the central office administrator is out to catch them. Being up front about the purpose and time of the visit will set the tone for a meaningful walkthrough.

Once the central office administrator arrives at the school, he or she needs to sit down with the principal and discuss the focus for the walkthrough. The building principal also needs to identify what he or she wants to look for during the walkthrough. The focus should be connected to the school's improvement and professional development plans. Aligning these processes needs to be discussed during the prebriefing. The prebriefing should typically last between 20–30 minutes.

During the supervisory walkthrough, the principal and central office administrator walk through the school and spend time talking to students, examining student work, and observing classroom lessons. Taking digital pictures or collecting student samples may also be appropriate during the walkthrough. It is important to get to as many classrooms as possible during the visit. If this isn't possible, the principal needs to decide which departments or wings need to be observed. The key issue here is to visit different areas of the building so as not to suggest to staff that only certain teachers or departments are responsible for improvement initiatives.

After supervisory walkthroughs, debriefings offer an opportunity to deepen the central office administrator's and the principal's reflections through dialogue. During the debriefing, the central office administrator asks open-ended questions that promote reflection and analysis from the principal. One technique that we frequently use is to draw a horizontal line in the middle of a piece of paper and explain that the line represents effective implementation of the look for. Then we ask the principal to identify what he or she observed that was above this line and what was below this line. Additional examples of open-ended questions to encourage reflection include "What were your general impressions regarding teaching and learning?" "What did you observe today that matched the look for?" "What did you observe today that was a close approximation of the look for?" and "Did you observe anything today that can be directly tied to your professional development plan?"

The final step in the supervisory walkthrough is the follow-up. During this step, principals write a letter to their staff that includes reflection from the visit. Typically, this letter includes thoughts or quotes from the central office administrator that validate effective practices observed. Although principals are responsible for providing feedback to their staff, the central office administrator needs to help principals by reviewing the letter and providing suggestions or feedback. In addition to providing support to building principals, the central office administrator may want to provide feedback in a letter or during principals' meetings. This feedback could include general observations about the teaching and learning throughout the district. This should occur after the central office administrator has completed a round of walkthroughs at a certain level. For example, after conducting walkthroughs at all the middle schools, it would be appropriate for the central office supervisor to write a letter to middle school principals validating the teaching and learning practices observed that met district goals. This type of feedback will help building principals develop a deeper understanding of the district goals, provide a model for giving feedback, and promote targeted instructional strategies.

## Power Tool: Collegial and Event Walkthroughs

The collegial walkthrough and the event walkthrough are used less frequently, yet they also help in monitoring school improvement efforts. Two peers or a mentor and protégé can use the collegial walkthrough together to observe teaching and learning in a school. This type of walkthrough helps develop professional relationships and can be particularly beneficial to new administrators. The procedures for the collegial walkthrough are similar to the supervisory walkthrough. The colleagues set up a scheduled visit and sit down and determine the focus for the walkthrough. Next, they walk through the building observing classrooms and talking to students. After classroom visits, they do a debriefing on their observations and identify any practices that met the look for. Suggestions and ideas are shared to address any concerns or areas that need improvement.

The event walkthrough takes place when a group of people observe the same teaching and learning experiences in a school building together. The purpose of the event walkthrough is to help teach the walkthrough process to principals or other instructional leaders through modeling. During the prebriefing for an event walkthrough the participants identify the look for of the day together to ensure that everyone is looking for the same thing. Without a predetermined focus, the group will only look for program results and not deep instructional strategies. A critical component for the event walkthrough is a group debriefing in which participants are asked to identify what they saw that matched the look for and to reflect on the walkthrough itself.

Another purpose for the event walkthrough is to help realign specific aspects of the curriculum. For example, in one school district, after conducting several supervisory walkthroughs, the central office administrator realized that students in elementary schools were assigned more rigorous and relevant writing assignments than students in middle and high schools. To help principals identify this issue, an event walkthrough was planned. K–12 administrators from the district came together and defined rigorous work. Administrators were divided into vertical teams and sent to two different buildings in the district to look for examples of rigor. The walkthroughs were organized so that principals did their observations in schools that were not at their same level (e.g., high school principals observed middle schools, and elementary school principals observed high schools). After spending time walking through several buildings, a debriefing session was held and administrators shared what they saw at each level. They discovered that the issue was watered-down writing assignments at the higher grade levels. The dialogue during the debriefing provided the team with an opportunity to address an issue that the district needed to face.

The event and collegial walkthrough can be very powerful tools if used correctly. There are some pitfalls to this process, and before venturing into these types of walkthroughs, several factors must be considered:

- **Pooling ignorance.** An event or collegial walkthrough will not be helpful if the person leading the walkthrough is not an astute instructional leader. This person also needs to know how to facilitate discussions during the debriefing to help identify the instructional issues that were observed. Without this type of leadership, the process turns into a feel-good walk around that does not get to the heart of teaching and learning issues. If the persons who are conducting the walkthroughs don't understand instruction, this process will simply pool the collective ignorance of the group. Before going down this road, it is critical to ensure that the participants and leader have a deep understanding of the most powerful teaching and learning strategies.

- **Lacking focus.** Without a clear focus, a collegial or an event walkthrough becomes a walk around. A lack of focus will manifest itself as tangential conversations about facilities, staffing, resources, or any issue outside of teaching and learning. A clear focus is paramount to the success of this process.
- **Lacking skills for giving and receiving feedback.** The power of this process lies in the conversations that participants have after the walkthrough. After a collegial or event walkthrough, participants need to be able to identify what is working and what needs to be worked on. If these things cannot be identified and shared, the process is meaningless.

Figure 7.5 provides a comparison of the purposes and procedures for event and collegial walkthroughs.

FIGURE 7.5 **Comparing Collegial and Event Walkthroughs**

| | Collegial | Event |
|---|---|---|
| **Purpose** | • Participants develop instructional leadership skills<br>• Participants solidify professional relationships<br>• Participants learn from each other | • Facilitator models the walkthrough process<br>• Facilitator identifies any vertical alignment issues |
| **Procedures** | • Participants receive an orientation on the school, demographics, and school improvement initiatives<br>• Host principal identifies the focus and the look fors<br>• Participants walk through the school<br>• Participants debrief on the walkthrough and share ideas<br>• Host principal provides feedback | • Facilitator conducts a prebriefing and gathers group consensus on the look for of the day<br>• Participants receive an orientation on the school, demographics, and school improvement initiatives<br>• Participants and facilitator walk through the school together<br>• Participants and facilitator debrief and share thoughts on the look for<br>• Central office administrator provides feedback to the facilitator and the host building |

## How Does Differentiated Personnel Supervision Support Alignment of the Blueprint Processes?

What is differentiated supervision for personnel? Certainly, school administrators and teachers know that supervising personnel includes evaluating teachers and determining processes for reemployment and formative improvement. But what would that process look like if it were differentiated for each person based on his or her individual needs? What if supervisors realized that teachers mature at different rates and stages that are not necessarily associated with years of service? Differentiated supervision embraces a different philosophy that is designed to match the level of supervision with the needs and competencies of individuals.

### A Framework for Differentiating Supervision

Charlotte Danielson and Thomas McGreal (2000) outline fresh approaches to teacher evaluation that build on what we now know about collaborative structures and adult learning. They propose a structural framework for teacher evaluation that includes multiple sources of data and a variety of professional activities and processes. One size does not fit all in this framework. One tier outlines procedures for evaluating beginning teachers, teachers who are new to a district, and tenured teachers. A second tier supports teachers who are engaged in professional development and growing in their own designs for improving their practice. A third tier provides assistance for teachers who need more help to meet performance expectations. Teachers are not assigned to these tracks based on job experience. Instead, teachers are assigned to tiers based on what they need to improve to influence student learning.

Differentiated supervision of personnel means that school leaders need to do things differently based on what individual teachers need and what students deserve. Both school and central office administrators need to be courageous when applying this concept. It is one thing to produce an evaluation document with different levels of supervision; it is quite another thing for a principal to tell a tenured teacher that he is in a track designed for novice teachers. Evaluating personnel to improve teaching requires both courage and adhering to procedures. Both processes are necessary to align personnel supervision with the other processes for school improvement.

## Aligning Supervision with the Blueprint Processes

Alignment for supervision involves selecting criteria for the district's evaluation system and matching the focus for observation, feedback, and evaluation options to specific goals for the school and district.

Danielson and McGreal (2000) clearly state that "the cornerstone of any evaluation system is the set of evaluative criteria on which a school or district bases its teacher evaluations." In the same way that well-constructed look fors clarify what is expected for implementing any innovation, principals and teachers need a set of criteria that can help them engage in dialogue about improving teaching and reach toward high-quality standards. Alignment occurs when the criteria selected for the district's evaluation list are compatible with the values, beliefs, and mission of the school. For example, Charlotte Danielson's (1996) framework for teaching includes an element of creating instructional groups as a part of designing coherent instruction. In this framework, proficient teachers use instructional groups that are varied according to curriculum goals and student needs. These criteria support a belief that learning occurs within a social context and that grouping students in a variety of ways promotes interactions that further their thinking.

Alignment occurs when the criteria for evaluation match what school leaders and teachers believe about teaching and learning. When these beliefs are out of alignment, the evaluation system is more vulnerable to mundane and perfunctory use. School leaders need to examine the criteria for teacher evaluation in light of the district mission, values, and beliefs as well as what is known about excellence in teaching.

School leaders also need to align dialogue about supervision with the other blueprint processes. For example, a school determines from data analysis that reading comprehension is an area where students need to improve. The faculty studies strategies that proficient readers can use to comprehend text and determines ways that they can embed those reading strategies across the curriculum. Next, school leaders determine that reading comprehension will become a strategy in the school improvement and professional development plans for raising achievement in literacy. Data to show the level of implementation and student learning outcomes are also collected to evaluate progress. All of these steps demonstrate how supervision can be aligned with other blueprint processes. Alignment for supervision also includes dialogue to increase accountability and productivity.

## Aligning Supervision with Dialogue

School leaders can promote dialogue about aligning supervision by providing walkthrough feedback, participating in classroom observations, and monitoring teacher evaluation systems.

Walkthrough feedback becomes an alignment tool when the discussions during and after classroom visits focus directly on issues that are related to the school improvement and professional development plans. If school leaders do not reference the goals and strategies in the school improvement plan, teachers have little hope of using the strategies to effect student learning. School leaders should avoid generic or prescriptive walkthrough feedback forms that are not directly tied to the school improvement or professional development plans. Formal methods for providing walkthrough feedback, such as writing a letter or memo to the staff, or informal methods, such as conversations, yield the best results for teachers when the feedback is tied to the same goals and expectations that teachers are working toward.

Classroom observation plays a major role in teacher evaluation systems. Regardless of the criteria or specific process used, evaluating teachers inevitably involves observing and reflecting on teaching methods in an actual classroom. Observing authentic teaching provides enormous potential for aligning all the blueprint processes together. Principals and central office supervisors must work with teachers to establish fair expectations for their observations. For example, in Nancy's early experiences as a young principal, she worked with a teacher evaluation system that required principals to do a specified number of scheduled and unscheduled observations. For the scheduled observations, teachers selected lessons that they wanted the principal to see. Most of Nancy's observations were more like stage performances than authentic lessons. In Nancy's situation, her feedback was rarely aligned with the school's goals or professional development focus. Her observations and her evaluations would have been more efficient if the content of the lesson were matched to the school's improvement goals and professional development efforts.

Classroom observations are most effective when principals and teachers work together to establish targeted areas for observation that match the school's goals and professional development efforts. Principals need to be fair and select areas to observe in which teachers have had sufficient opportunity to learn and practice an innovation. When principals and teachers create a climate of trust and respect, they eliminate a "gotcha" approach for classroom observation, and they can develop a sharper focus on school improvement.

Modern teacher evaluation systems provide multiple sources of data to document teacher performance. Classroom observations, portfolios, artifact collections, and student data are great sources to gather for evaluation. To align her school's data collection with their professional development efforts, Principal Jeaneen Boyer from St. Joseph, Missouri, asks her teachers to collect artifacts such as reading and writing conference notes as evidence that they are implementing a workshop approach to literacy. These artifacts document teachers' growth and development and show principals how the professional development efforts are working in classrooms. Thus, teachers' evaluations are not separated from what teachers are doing to improve the school.

## Power Tool: The Postobservation Conference

In an earlier scenario, we talked about Nancy's early teacher evaluations and how they were not connected to the school improvement plan or professional development focus. Likewise, her conversations after the evaluations were not aligned with the school's improvement efforts because they were focused on her district's pre-established criteria for teacher evaluation. The result was a mixed potpourri of suggestions, observations, reinforcements, and questions.

Postobservation conferences should be aligned with the blueprint processes to improve teaching and student learning. The conference itself is not a power tool unless the structure and form of the conference align with all other aspects of school improvement.

### Postobservation Conference Goals

What is the purpose of a postobservation conversation? The answer depends largely on how leaders supervise their staff members. There are many models for conducting these conversations. Edward Pajak (2000) says, "Those who have responsibility for observing classrooms and providing feedback…may be unclear about how best to accomplish these tasks and about the advice that various experts in the field have to offer." There are clinical approaches to supervision that range from original models by Goldhammer (1969) and Cogan (1973) to humanistic models from Blumberg (1974) to technical models by Hunter (1986) and Joyce and Showers (1982). There are also developmental and reflective models from Glickman (1985) and Costa and Garmston (1985). The purpose of the postobservation discussion depends on the needs of the teacher, the requirements of the evaluation system, and the overall approach taken towards supervision.

We favor a clinical supervision approach that has a postobservation conference framework that can be adapted to fit a variety of conference goals. The conference should be differentiated to meet the needs of the individual teacher. The framework we like to use is modified from a model created by Madeline Hunter (1986). It provides a skeletal outline from which principals can prepare for the conversation and keep it focused. Principals can also use the gradual release of responsibility model for their conversations to help teachers improve specific teaching behaviors based on the maturity and ability of the teacher. The more reflective the teacher is, the less directive the principal needs to be. The goal of the conversation is to align teaching improvement efforts with the mission, beliefs, values, and goals for the school. By using a framework with the conversation, principals and teachers can focus their efforts on a specific set of goals.

## The Postobservation Framework

A postobservation framework includes several parts that can be modified based on the overall goal of the conversation:

- **Introduction.** A postobservational conversation should begin with an introduction that is cordial, sincere, and relational. This introduction should not be a greeting that quickly turns into a heavy discussion about teaching. An effective introduction fosters the climate of trust and respect.
- **Reflection and Gathering Information.** This conversation should also include time for reflection and gathering information. This time will allow the supervisor to listen to the teacher's perspective on his or her strengths in teaching and any areas that need refinement. This part of the conference can easily become a mundane recitation of the teacher's strengths and weaknesses; however, at this point, the principals should use this time to ask focused questions to foster reflection and to listen intently for the teacher's insights.
- **Recognizing Strengths.** Pointing out teachers' strengths helps them to continue using these effective teaching behaviors. While recognizing teachers' accomplishments is important, two common problems can occur. One problem is reciting a laundry list of good teaching behaviors that are too long to remember after the conference, and the second issue is providing feedback that sounds artificial or generic. Principals should select one or two strengths

that will encourage teachers and will have the greatest influence on learning and the school's professional development efforts.

- **Identifying Improvements.** Principals also need to use this conversation to confront any behaviors or practices that need improving. Principals should pick one area for improvement that has the greatest chance of influencing student learning. Identifying too many refinements or sugarcoating the need for improvement defeats the purpose of this part of the conference.
- **Checking for Understanding.** Throughout the conference, the principal should ensure that the teacher's understanding of the conference matches his or her own perspective. The principal should ask the teacher to rephrase big ideas about his or her strengths and improvements. This part of the conversation should sound conversational rather than like a pop quiz.
- **Creating Summary Statements.** The conference concludes with summary statements. Typically, principals will provide forms that need to be shared or signed and they will give teachers the next steps, which include a timeline for future actions.

From Nancy's experiences, she believes that school principals need a basic framework for planning a conversation, opportunities to practice and receive feedback on using frameworks, and freedom to adapt this framework to fit varying supervisory needs. Reflection and self-assessment greatly increase the chances for teachers' growth beyond the postobservation conversation.

Supervising teaching, learning, and people clearly fits in a framework for school improvement. Principals and supervisors need to have established criteria for implementing professional development to maintain standards of excellence. Supervision that is not aligned with other blueprint processes merely adds another task to the already overloaded plate of school principals and hard-working teachers.

## Reflections from the Field

For over 30 years, Nancy's husband has crafted custom-made saddles and Western riding equipment. Every saddle is made to fit the horse and its rider. Horse trailers pull up outside the saddlery, and customers unload their favorite steed so that the saddle maker can measure and fit the saddle to just the right proportions. A Mooney saddle is guaranteed to fit. One size doesn't fit all.

Likewise, as we supervise teachers, we customize the best fit for monitoring and giving them feedback to improve teaching. We have to special order our supervision to match the needs of the teachers. One size doesn't fit all. Even our formal evaluation process needs to match the needs of the teachers. For far too long, school districts have tried to cram a wide range of developmental levels into one evaluation system. Differentiating supervision should be considered in the same way that we would want teachers to differentiate instruction to meet the needs of a wide range of students. Some teachers need close monitoring using a clinical supervision model, while other teachers need projects and professional development followed by reflection. Yet another group of teachers may need to create their own horizons and evaluate themselves with a coach or a mentor. The possibilities are out there if we fit the system to the needs of the teachers.

A fundamental part of any system is the feedback. It doesn't matter how many levels or tracks of evaluation make up the system if principals lack the courage to give teachers honest feedback that fosters deep reflection on teaching practices. Good saddle making requires feedback from the buyer and the horse to get the proper fit. Good supervision that improves teaching and learning requires feedback matched to the school's goals and the individual's needs.

—Nancy Mooney

## Touchstone Texts

Blasé, J., & Blasé, J. (1998). *Handbook of instructional leadership: How really good principals promote teaching and learning.* Thousand Oaks, CA: Corwin Press.

Danielson, C. (1996). *Enhancing professional practice: A framework for teaching.* Alexandria, VA: ASCD.

Danielson, C., & McGreal, T. (2000). *Teacher evaluation to enhance professional practice.* Alexandria, VA: ASCD.

Evans, R. (1996). *The human side of change.* San Francisco: Jossey-Bass.

Platt, A., Tripp, C., Ogden, W., & Fraser, R. (2000). *The skillful leader: Confronting mediocre teaching.* Acton, MA: The Ready Press.

Whitaker, T. (1999). *Dealing with difficult teachers.* Larchmont, NY: Eye on Education.

# 8

# Creating Leaders for School Improvement

There can be no significant learning without significant relationships.

—*James Comer*

The purpose of this chapter is to clarify our position on essential aspects of leadership. The professional literature on leadership offers far more than we can convey in this book. Instead, we seek to point out those aspects of leadership that we value the most in our work of implementing the blueprint processes. Aligning the blueprint processes to fundamental characteristics of leadership increases the possibility that teachers can fully implement school improvement processes in their classrooms. Without leadership, the blueprint processes are void of the human dynamics that are required to get school improvement initiatives off the paper and into the classroom.

## Essential Questions

- Who does a leader need to be as a person?
- What does a leader need to do to demonstrate leadership?

These questions address who the leader needs to be and what the leader needs to do. The first essential question asks about the inner qualities and characteristics that leaders need for good leadership. Three characteristics that we believe stand out for good leaders are having strong character, being a learner, and establishing relationships of trust and respect. The second essential question asks how leaders can use their actions to make their leadership position more than just a job or an elusive ideal. We believe that the leader's actions include developing the capacity of others, sharing governance, communicating effectively, and following a plan that is consistent with one's vision and mission.

## Three Dimensions of Leadership

*The American President* is a movie that tells the story of a widowed president who pursues a romantic relationship with a lobbyist. Near the end of the movie, President Andrew Shepherd unexpectedly enters the White House pressroom to speak out about character attacks levied at him by his political opponents. He opens his speech by saying, "Being president of the United States is entirely about character." He goes on to say that individuals of strong character are distinguished by integrity, honesty, and forthrightness. While this scene is from a fictional movie, these themes of character and leadership ring true. Whether leading a school, a district, or a nation, leadership is entirely about character. Leaders also need to be lifelong learners, and they need to be open to building relationships. Educational leaders, in particular, need to continually seek learning as a means of improving themselves and their organizations.

## Essential Characteristics for Educational Leadership

Thomas Sergiovanni (2000) notes that "character is the defining characteristic of authentic leadership." A laundry list of desirable traits accompanies the literature on leadership, including honesty, caring, integrity, patience, trustworthiness, dependability, commitment, responsibility, and honor (Council of Chief State School Officers, 1996; Heifeitz, 1994; Lambert, 1998; Marzano et al., 2005; NAESP, 1997; Tomlinson, 2000). Which of these characteristics truly define a good leader? Are all of these virtues required for success in leadership? Is there a formula, flow chart, or framework for building character?

The three characteristics that we believe distinguish good leaders are integrity, courage, and compassion. All three characteristics can be developed when a leader puts forth the effort and energy to include these characteristics in his or her personality. The caveat for this development is that the leader must make a conscious choice to change and mature. These types of changes don't happen by participating in character development programs or by attempting to demonstrate behaviors that are not a true reflection of a person's character. Leaders with strong character choose to live, work, and maintain their values amid the turmoils of leadership. People of great character never compromise their integrity or compassion for selfish purposes. Their leadership reflects their character.

### Integrity

Robert Evans (1996) defines integrity as a fundamental consistency among one's values, goals, and actions. People with enormous integrity can be counted on to be what they say and to do what they profess to believe. To say one thing and do another signals a lack of integrity that erodes the confidence and trust that followers have in their leader. Leaders with integrity stand by their words and instill confidence in their staff members by following through on their actions. These types of leaders know how to be patient and wait for information so that they can make good decisions. Leaders with integrity are honest with themselves and their staff members, and their commitment matches their beliefs, words, and actions.

### Courage

Jim Collins (2001) describes five levels of leadership in his research on the differences between good and great companies. He says that Level 5 leaders are " [leaders who are] resolved to do whatever it takes to make the company great, no matter how big or hard the decisions." Doing whatever it takes demands that leaders have the courage to forge ahead to get results despite hardships, discouragement, or resistance. All too often, courage is equated with leaders who are fearless in the face of incredible odds. Courage in educational leadership is not the absence of fear but the willingness to put proven processes into action. Courageous leaders look at all the risks, and they are willing to stay the course to fully implement good processes that improve schools and students. These leaders fully live their beliefs, and they demonstrate courage whether the decisions are big or small. Courageous leaders also hold themselves and others accountable, continually seek feedback from their staff members, spend time reflecting on their leadership, and know when to let others lead.

### Compassion

Compassionate leaders view themselves as servants, and they exhibit humility and care for the people that they lead. Collins (2001) describes Level 5 leaders as "a paradoxical mix of personal humility and professional will." He discovered that leaders of great companies were more interested in the company than themselves. Compassionate leaders serve others so that the vision and mission of the organization can manifest into reality. Educational leaders strive to make school improvement become a reality. When leaders care deeply about serving others, their compassion builds up the character of those they serve. Think about a person with great compassion. His or her caring and servant attitude creates relationships of trust and respect. It is much easier to trust someone who seeks to serve your best interests and stands with you in times of trouble or uncertainty.

Blanchard and Hodges (2003) say, "[Servant leadership] requires a level of intimacy with the needs and aspirations of the people that might be beyond the level of intimacy an ego-driven leader is willing to sustain." Compassionate leaders care enough to hold their followers accountable. Don't confuse compassion with permissiveness. Servant leaders expect those they serve to maintain high standards and to be accountable; however, they are sensitive to the sacrifices their staff members may need to make to achieve a goal. Compassionate leaders offer continuous assistance, persistent encouragement, and unbridled praise for work well done.

## Being a Lifelong Learner

Superintendent Melody Smith (2006) opened her school year convocation meeting with a stirring challenge for teachers and administrators. She challenged her audience with a question that conveys the essence of lifelong learning for adults in schools. She said, "Children grapple with new information every day. Is it too much to ask that I should do the same thing?" Superintendent Smith continued her speech by acknowledging that learning is a messy process that seldom comes without inconsistencies or questions. She observed that this messy learning often comes with a feeling of discomfort, but lifelong learners persist and go on to discover what works for schools and students.

Leaders who are lifelong learners stay ahead of the pack by studying effective practices and processes and measuring the efficacy of any practice with their own beliefs and values. Central office leaders who are in charge of curriculum, instruction, and assessment should continually seek to learn new information that goes beyond the latest trends and patterns in the profession. These leaders need to focus on practices that improve teaching and learning in their district and help them to build their own professional insights. Likewise, principals need to embrace continuous learning by sitting in the front row in professional development sessions and eagerly reading and discussing professional literature. Continual learning also includes studying new ideas, trends, and insights and revisiting bedrock principles of teaching and learning. Lifelong learning is messy, but committed leaders know that thoroughly learning the practices and processes that drive school improvement will lead to better schools and higher achievement for students.

## Establishing Relationships

Nancy frequently opens her talks about school improvement by saying, "It's all about relationships." If the blueprint processes described throughout this book and in other literature lead to improvement, then how can school improvement be all about relationships? The answer is that schools consist of people, both adults and children.

People operate within a web of relationships, and these relationships create the fabric of the school. Without relationships in schools, there are only processes. It's the people who make the processes come alive. If people don't have relationships with one another, no school improvement process can have sustained improvement.

What kinds of relationships foster great school improvement? One fundamental condition is a relationship built on trust. A relationship built on trust creates a safe and supportive environment that fosters communication, reflection, and growth. The absence of mutual trust creates an environment of fear. In organizations built around fear, individuals are more focused on personal agendas rather than working toward a common goal. Relationships of mistrust undermine school improvement efforts because they divert attention away from important issues such as student achievement.

Developing trust takes time, and leaders can build trust with their staff members by their actions. Leaders also need to be aware that cultivating trusting relationships can sometimes get pushed aside in pursuit of other school improvement goals; however, school leaders need to understand that no matter how pressing a school initiative is, they cannot accomplish the task alone. Doug Reeves (2006) says, "We survive as a species and as leaders of an organization not due to solitary efforts but due to organizational and collaborative success" (p. 26). The success of school improvement efforts are based on relationships that are cultivated by the leader. Leadership practices that create and enhance trusting relationships include the following:

- **Listening.** Everyone has something to say and wants to be heard. Even if a leader has a strong and distinct vision for the school or district, it is imperative to listen and hear what the group has to say. Listening validates the speaker and helps the leader assess the current situation and figure out the next steps for school improvement.
- **Follow-through.** Leaders need to follow through on what they say they are going to do. Nothing destroys trust faster than letting someone down. Leaders often have the tendency to want to do all and be all for their staff members; however, they need to recognize that it is impossible to do everything. A good leader focuses on the school's priorities and follows through on activities that will have the greatest impact on student achievement.
- **Openness.** Relationships that work are reciprocal. Leaders must reveal parts of themselves if they want their staff members to share their concerns and issues. Open leaders are not afraid to admit mistakes or implement ideas that are not their own. Open leaders do not have any hidden agendas, and their staff knows and understands where the school or district is headed and why.

Once trusting relationships are developed, it is much easier for the leader to work with staff members who need constructive feedback. The leader who understands that people are more important than things understands that improving organizations often includes redirecting people. Just as good parents have to redirect and confront their children when they are not doing what they need to do, a good leader must do the same. It may be difficult to approach staff members who need to improve, but not doing so jeopardizes the relationship and their performance. Working with difficult staff members is never easy, but for the leader who knows how to develop relationships, the task can be less daunting.

## Four Dimensions of Leadership Work

Implementing the blueprint processes and the power tools associated with each process constitutes a major portion of the work leaders do to improve schools. For leaders who seek to go beyond good leadership to demonstrate great and lasting leadership, four additional aspects of leadership work overlap the blueprint processes. These processes include developing the capacity of others, sharing governance, leading by communicating, and living by a vision.

## Developing the Capacity of Others

Leadership books, courses, and seminars frequently focus on behaviors that leaders engage in to increase success or efficiency. In his book *Good to Great*, Jim Collins (2001) reveals that great companies are led by people who are more servant oriented than charismatic. Charismatic leaders are capable of moving an organization forward, but they don't equip others to keep the organization's success going once the leaders step aside. Collins says, "Good leaders want to see the company even more successful in the next generation, [and they are] comfortable with the idea that most people won't even know that the roots of that success trace back to their efforts." We believe that leaders should make plans to move the organization forward for both the present and the future. Enlarging leadership capacity means that the leaders open up avenues for other staff members to emerge as leaders and expand the organization's mission and vision.

Building staff capacity expands the definition of who can lead and roots out ineffective paradigms about how staff members can become principals, central office leaders, or teacher leaders. Capacity building also creates opportunities for staff members to gain the knowledge, skills, and attitudes that are necessary to put the blueprint processes in place. Developing capacity requires leaders to create intense, focused professional development opportunities and to encourage their staff members to devote more time to questioning and reflection.

### Professional Development for School Leaders

School and district leaders who are serious about long-term improvement begin implementing the blueprint processes by developing their leaders. Providing professional development for school leaders builds the capacity of central office administrators, principals, and teacher leaders so that school improvement can continue when leadership transitions occur. Building capacity for all leaders emphasizes that the mission and vision are more important than the work of a single leader. School and district leaders need to invest in building capacity for all three levels of leadership.

**1. Central office leadership development.** Central office leaders who are in charge of instruction have the greatest need to develop their knowledge and skills regarding teaching, learning, and leadership. Professional development at this level must be more than attending national conventions or workshops. Central office leaders need focused study on topics that either raise the current level of achievement within the district curriculum or promote thinking about the next level for district improvement. These leaders also need mentoring and contact with networks of trusted colleagues with similar jobs in other districts. Central office leaders can benefit from talking to people who can give them an unbiased view of their district, data, and climate. Central office administrators shouldn't hoard their findings for fear of giving their competition an edge. If medical science hoarded information the way that educators do, only a few people would benefit from the enormous leaps in medicine.

**2. Principal development.** The greatest single investment a district can make for school improvement is professional development for principals. Principals must be smart about teaching and learning in order to raise the bar for students and teachers. They need to know about the best practices and how to implement them. Professional development for principals needs to be focused on pedagogy and practice. When principals can have a dialogue about practical applications, they can develop the knowledge and skills that are necessary to sustain instructional improvement. Districts can use a variety of professional development methods for principals including monthly principal meetings devoted to professional development, study groups, mentoring, and principals' academies or cohort groups.

The Western Pennsylvania Principal Academy in Pittsburgh, Pennsylvania is a powerful example of an academy format that transforms instructional leaders. For over 25 years, academy directors Joseph Werlinich and Otto Graf have provided networking opportunities for principals from all levels and experience. A systematic evaluation of this academy shows that participants highly value the mentoring relationship that they develop with the directors and the opportunity to have sustained dialogue with other principals about practical topics about the principalship. When Nancy directed cohorts of new principals and assistant principals, she discovered that principals' academies have the most power when they are connected with practical strategies for leadership and the blueprint processes. Principals benefit from academies and cohorts because they have devoted time to study, network, and have open dialogue with their colleagues.

Monthly principals' meetings that are devoted to raising principals' knowledge of curriculum and instruction are also powerful methods for professional development. Most of the managerial tasks that are discussed at administrative meetings can be handled by other means of communication. This precious time that principals have away from their schools needs to be focused on content that has the greatest chance of influencing student learning. We are not suggesting that leaders ignore noninstructional concerns at principals' meetings. Instead, leaders can address many of these concerns by using written communication. Putting professional development first establishes a sense of urgency for student achievement.

**3. Teacher leader development.** Building capacity for shared governance and leadership also includes investing in teachers as leaders. A teacher's job demands incredible knowledge and skill that may not include all the necessary elements for effective leadership. Teachers need to develop skills for facilitation, coaching, mentoring other teachers, sharing governance, analyzing data, and resolving conflicts. Teachers also need training for all the blueprint processes to ensure that every faculty member contributes to full alignment and implementation. Teachers can use summer institutes, study groups, cohorts, and off-site professional development for leadership training. Department chairs, members of professional development committees, and building leadership teams can conduct leadership training for teachers. Strong teacher leaders coupled with highly skilled principals set the stage for powerful shared leadership.

### Devoting Time for Questioning and Reflection

Asking questions builds leaders' capacity, and reflection deepens their understanding. For example, central office supervisors who ask principals reflective questions before jumping in with advice reap two benefits. First, principals answer the questions based on solutions that they have created with their supervisor. This helps to reinforce their commitment to implementing the solution. Second, principals walk away with more than just an answer to a single problem. They now have multiple strategies for solving future concerns.

In another example, a principal might call his or her central office supervisor to discuss a teacher's performance on implementing a part of the curriculum. The principal poses the problem and asks the supervisor, "What should I do?" At this point, the supervisor may be tempted to become "Mr. or Ms. Fix It" and solve the problem to serve the needs of the principal and the situation. While jumping in to help will solve the problem, a valuable opportunity for building capacity slips away. Instead, the supervisor should guide the principal toward carefully using reflective questioning and should release authority to allow principals to make decisions on their own. Allowing principals to develop their own solutions will help them to improve their current situation and develop strategies for solving future issues.

Reflective questioning becomes especially important during a supervisory walkthrough. Central office supervisors should use the walkthrough to teach principals, build their capacity for instructional leadership, and ask hard questions that require thoughtful answers. Supervisors who stroll through a school whipping off criticisms and unsolicited advice, even if it is warranted, are not building instructional leaders who can upgrade the quality of teaching and learning in their schools. Likewise, principals should also ask teachers reflective questions to help them foster deeper thinking and understanding. Devoting time for questioning and reflection allows central office leaders, principals, and teachers to enlarge and expand their vision for what is possible within the organization.

## Sharing Governance

Multiplying power builds capacity and expands the organization's opportunities for more innovations in teaching and learning. Jo and Joseph Blasé (1997) agree with the idea of expanding school governance and say, "Principals who embrace teacher professionalism do more than share power: They multiply it." Marzano and colleagues (2005) identified 21 responsibilities for school leaders and their effects on student achievement. Several of these concepts, including involving teachers in decisions, being flexible, and working with dissention and change, have positive correlations with school and student achievement and sharing governance. Operating in an organization that shares governance means that every person exercises democratic principles for decision making, honors each role and responsibility, and recognizes that every person contributes to the success of the organization.

It's amazing that on Inauguration Day in the United States, one person steps down from the most powerful job in the world, and another person takes over in a matter of minutes, without a coup, rebellion, military action, or rioting in the streets! This transfer of power is a built-in part of the democratic system, and it occurs despite differing points of view and serious philosophical rifts. How does this happen? Sharing governance allows power to be distributed and transferred based on mutual agreements that support the decision-making system. Rebellion is not necessary when democracy rules, but democracy comes with responsibilities, such as sharing the work and accountability and respecting differing points of view. Jo and Joseph Blasé (1997) identify four frustrations that occur when faculty members begin sharing governance. We have also observed these same frustrations in our schools and districts, and we added our own insights to these concepts. Being aware of these frustrations can help school leaders if and when these challenges emerge.

• **Create Time for Governance Work.** Both principals and teachers quickly find that sharing governance takes a lot of time. Autocratic leadership is efficient, and it only takes one person to make a decision. Democracy is slower and requires more time for every person to process the decision. Sometimes faculties and central office staff members just don't want to put in the time to make a democratic decision. Over the years, we have even heard our staff members say, "Just tell us what to do." While this suggestion is tempting, it seldom leads to the kind of empowerment that staff members need for self-governance. Ultimately, holding out for decisions that are made by using shared governance is worth it. Leaders should be prepared for initial resistance from their staff, and they should openly acknowledge the amount of hard work required to reach the goal.

• **Focus on Instruction.** When groups begin to share governance, there is a tendency for group members to select decisions that have minimal instructional impact. It is much easier for a group to decide the paint color for the teacher's lounge than to devise an intervention for struggling readers. As groups make the transition to shared leadership, they may choose to begin by practicing with smaller decisions and celebrate the process of making a shared decision. Next, they should expand their decision-making process to focus on goals from the school improvement and professional development plans. Leaders should continually remind the groups that the ultimate goal is improving student learning.

• **Make Groups Inclusive.** School leaders should select leadership groups that represent the whole organization and include individuals whose input is important for big decisions. District leaders also need to develop governance processes that encourage senior-level administrators to listen and seek insight from midlevel personnel. Everyone in the organization should share the burdens and joys of collective leadership.

• **Know How to Back Off.** The hardest part of transitioning to shared leadership is backing off from previous paradigms about who makes decisions. Changing the guard for leadership is a gradual process that is not accomplished with one swoop or announcement. Seasoned leaders may be scared to give up their decision-making authority, even if they have a few moments of celebration. Leaders should transition to shared leadership by backing off of their leadership responsibilities and building the capacity of their staff members. They should teach their staff members how and when to lead and give them feedback early in the process. Leaders should also know when to step in if a situation becomes challenging.

## Central Office Governance

Nearly all districts with multiple central office leaders use senior administrative leadership groups such as a superintendent's cabinet, superintendent's council, or superintendent's team. While the titles will vary from different districts and states, typically these groups are responsible for operating and leading major district functions such as human resources, finance, or curriculum and instruction. In larger districts, these groups also include department heads. In smaller districts, the cabinet or council usually consists of the superintendent, one or two district staff members, and principals. These groups are not unique; however, district groups and leaders should work toward creating a unique vision for shared leadership that includes trusting each other's perspectives, sharing the burdens and joys of leadership, and opening up conversations for different viewpoints.

Sharing governance at the district level means devising structures that include input from everyone. School leaders should also be sure to include personnel who are in supportive roles. These staff members often know a great deal about the inner workings of the district, and their knowledge and insight will help leaders spread and share valuable information throughout the district.

## School Governance

School leaders can begin implementing shared leadership by establishing a clear organizational governance system that can be tracked through a flowchart. The flowchart should represent an understood and agreed-upon sequence for decision making that is accepted by the entire school. Numerous school reform models such as Accelerated Schools, the Coalition of Essential Schools, and professional learning communities use democratic principles to help school leaders share the decision-making process (DuFour & Eaker, 1998; Finnan, et. al., 1995; Sizer,1997). School leaders need to choose or create a model that makes sense for the school, ensure that everyone knows the governance structure, and clarify who will be in charge of making decisions.

Next, school leaders must be truthful about how decisions are currently made in the school and how decisions should be made in an ideal vision of shared leadership. The differences between the two models will show school leaders and their staff members where they are as they make the transition into shared leadership. Figure 8.1 suggests ways that school leaders can initiate this discussion and develop a governance structure that helps their staff members move closer to their

**FIGURE 8.1 Decision Making and the Blueprint Processes**

| Blueprint Processes | NOW<br>Who currently makes the decision for each of these school improvement processes? | TRANSITION<br>How can the school begin to move to an ideal model for decision making? What transitional steps can be implemented immediately? | IDEAL VISION<br>What would decision making look like if it were done in an ideal fashion? What is our vision for decision making? |
|---|---|---|---|
| **Mission and Vision** | | | |
| **Data Analysis** | | | |
| **School Improvement Plan** | | | |
| **Professional Development Plan** | | | |
| **Supervising Teaching, Learning, and People** | | | |

desired vision for shared leadership. Finally, after school leaders select a decision-making structure, they can use the structure to delineate basic decisions and delegate assignments to their staff members.

## Leading by Communicating

The art of communication is the language of leadership.

—*James Humes*

Communication is the conduit that helps the leader develop and maintain relationships, reinforce the vision and mission for the school or district, and strengthen the focus for school improvement efforts. As essential as communication is to the leader, it can also be time-consuming and difficult work. Communicating frequently, honestly, consistently, and constructively is the key for doing leadership work. Although there isn't one foolproof method for providing communication as the leader, we have found a few tried-and-true methods that keep the lines of communication open and move the teaching and learning agenda forward.

## Power Tool: The Weekly Message

Sending a weekly message to staff is a common practice in many school buildings. Typically, these bulletins include a preview of the upcoming week's activities and announcements. Although it is important for the staff to know about the nuts and bolts of the school or organization, the weekly message is an opportunity to continually affirm and direct the teaching and learning initiatives in the organization. Thus, we advocate shifting the weekly message from a bulletin board message to a memo that conveys the teaching and learning initiatives in the school. Leaders should include the following items in their weekly communications:

- Thoughts and reflections on teaching and learning practices observed throughout the week
- Excerpts from articles on teaching and learning that include suggestions or ideas for incorporating the practices into the organization
- Revisiting or clarifying the vision and mission
- Updating progress on the school improvement and professional development plans

When a leader begins using a weekly message, two major things happen. First, the message conveys what the leader believes are the most important issues in the school. Communicating these ideas is a critical step for leaders as they work toward developing relationships with their staff members. Nuts and bolts items need to be discussed as well, but if all that the staff ever reads about are dismissal procedures or book order deadlines, then management issues will take precedence over the real work of teaching and learning. Second, the weekly message provides the leader with an opportunity to shape and revisit the school improvement initiatives. Staff members need ongoing feedback and direction to accomplish real change in student achievement. The regular message is an important tool that can help get this job done.

In our roles as central office leaders, we both use weekly messages to regularly communicate with principals. The "Reflections from the Field" at the end of each chapter are excerpts from the Mooney Memo and Mausbach Message. We used this communiqué as an opportunity to provide regular and ongoing information to a large audience. As a central office administrator, it is impossible to be in every school as often as one would like. The weekly message allows central office leaders to have an exchange of ideas with the principals and school leaders whom they supervise. Ann Weston, a principal in the St. Joseph School District in St. Joseph, Missouri, once said to Nancy "Reading the Mooney Memo is like having a conversation with you. I know what you are thinking." One of the first things that Ann did when she was responsible for curriculum and instruction in 60 elementary schools was to institute the Mausbach Message. This was one of the first opportunities that the principals had to understand who Ann was as a leader and to discuss the teaching and learning practices that needed to be addressed throughout the district.

In addition to helping leaders develop relationships, the weekly message also serves as a one-stop shop for the district's basic communication needs. Rather than having every department bombard principals with e-mails that contain deadlines and notices, the weekly message from central office consolidates this information into one document. Weekly messages from the central office can include the following components:

- Announcements and updates from major departments in the district, such as human resources and support services
- Upcoming deadlines and scheduled meetings for the week
- Updates on curriculum and instruction
- Clarifications on any curriculum changes
- Reflections on teaching and learning practices
- Excerpts from articles on teaching and learning

Sending the weekly message out on the same day each week helps principals manage their responsibilities and gives them a consistent mode for communicating information. Providing a consolidated and consistent document is another way for central office leaders to serve and support school leaders. Examples of the Mooney Memo and Mausbach Message can be found in Appendix F (see p. 184).

## Living by a Vision

Leaders who live by a vision go beyond knowing where they want to go; they also use an internal compass that directs their actions and decision making. There is a subtle but critical distinction between establishing a vision and living by a vision. Principals are not living by a vision when they purport that the mission for their school is teaching and learning, yet they allow classes to be interrupted throughout the day for noninstructional announcements. Leaders are not living by a vision when they say that all students can learn, but they have a myriad of excuses when achievement does not improve.

Leaders who live by a vision know what they stand for, and they align their actions with their beliefs. If leaders have a vision that all students can learn, they will work toward developing programs and systems to make this vision a reality, even when they are faced with challenges. Leaders who believe that all students deserve a first-class education will spend considerable time and energy developing their staff members to ensure that every teacher is highly qualified. Moving an organization forward is difficult work, but for the leader who doesn't live by a vision, the task is nearly impossible.

The vision for a school or district should be fluid. As the leader evolves, so does the vision. This doesn't mean that leaders should abandon the vision for the latest trend; the vision will deepen and expand as the leader grows and develops. Effective leaders are continually learning, growing, and seeking new information and processes to achieve their goals. Their vision will be naturally shaped by this process. For example, if leaders believe that writing is essential to student achievement, they may start by working with their staff members to use specific strategies to incorporate writing across all the content areas. Over time, principals may realize that writing achievement improves when a workshop approach to instruction is used. Thus, their vision for writing instruction wasn't abandoned, it was simply extended for better results.

Richard Wallace, superintendent emeritus of the Pittsburgh school district, coined the phrase "focus–follow-up–finish" to define what he believes are the determining factors for successful school reform. He notes that the difference between schools and districts that achieve improved performance and those that don't is the ability to intensely focus on one or more aspects of teaching and learning. After a focus has been determined, leaders follow-up with their staff members to ensure that they are continuing to implement an initiative. Finally, districts and schools that succeed at improving their schools have leaders who get to the finish line because they stick to their vision. Regardless of the school improvement strategy, the "focus–follow-up–finish" strategy will help leaders move toward a path for success. Good leaders don't abandon their staff or move on to the next initiative until every child benefits from the innovation.

## Reflections from the Field

I vividly recall waking up on a bright Saturday morning after the whirlwind week in which I was appointed as a new principal by the board of education. Everything seemed to be going my way. I received congratulations from my family, colleagues, and the community, and I felt on top of the world. Then I woke up on Saturday morning with a looming question in my head and an ache in the pit of my stomach. I remember thinking, "Oh my goodness! I got the job. Now what do I do?" Perhaps you have had a similar experience of working hard to reach a goal, and then suddenly you find yourself wondering what to do, even though you have the fundamental knowledge and skills to succeed.

Since that time, it has been my great privilege to be the direct supervisor for a dozen new administrators during their first year as a principal. Inevitably, during our first orientation, a principal will ask, "What is the most important thing to do first?" Each person asks the question in a different way, but the question is the same. Several principals have even phrased it by saying, "Now that I have the job, what do I do first?" My Saturday morning experience has served me well.

So, what is the most important thing for principals to do first, given the enormity of their job? My advice to new principals is the same advice that I give to the most seasoned veteran: *the most important thing is to build relationships. I tell new principals: Join with students, parents, faculty, and colleagues to build trusting relationships and develop genuine care and concern for those whom you serve. Get to know the people around you and discover how you can meet their needs and understand their concerns.*

*There are powerful processes and tools that exist to improve schools. Data analysis, strategic planning, professional development, and differentiated supervision combine to produce real reform for school improvement. But relationships of trust and respect are the bedrock on which those processes and tools stand. What do you do first? Build relationships.*

*—Nancy Mooney*

## Touchstone Texts

Blanchard, K., & Hodges, P. (2003). *The servant leader: Transforming your heart, head, hands, and habits*. Nashville, TN: J. Countryman.

Blasé, J., & Blasé, J. (1997). *The fire is back! Principals sharing school governance*. Thousands Oaks, CA: Corwin Press.

Collins, J. (2001). *Good to great*. New York: HarperCollins Business.

Evans, R. (1996). *The human side of school change*. San Francisco: Jossey-Bass.

# Appendix A
# Sample State of the Schools Report

**Achievement City Public Schools**
**State of Elementary Schools**
**2001–02**
**MASTERCRAFT[1]—Mathematics**

## Background and Rationale

MASTERCRAFT is a software program that fosters the development of K–12 articulated curriculum goals that match national, state, and local standards and the development of local assessments to measure student learning. MASTERCRAFT software was put into use in Anytown for the first time during the 1998–99 school year. The area of mathematics was targeted as the first K–12 articulated curriculum, meaning that the goals for students at all grade levels are matched in a way that permits a continuous flow of instructional expectations from kindergarten through graduation.

The MASTERCRAFT math tests were created locally by selecting key math goals at each grade level and choosing test items that measure that goal. A multiple-choice format was used for the first administration of MASTERCRAFT math. This format matches the Terra Nova portion of the Missouri Assessment Program (MAP) tests given in mathematics at grades 4, 8, and 10. Performance items will be added in future administrations of this test.

[1]MASTERCRAFT is a fictional program.

The MASTERCRAFT tests are not standardized evaluations in the sense that they compare Anytown students to students in other school districts in Missouri or nationally. The items were selected to assess specific goals and objectives that are a part of the mathematics curriculum at the tested grade level. A level of content validity is therefore inherent in the test design because the items tested have been verified to match the content of the curriculum at the appropriate grade level. All students at a grade level take the same MASTERCRAFT test.

## Purposes of the MASTERCRAFT Math Assessment

1. To give feedback to administrators, teachers, and students on levels of mathematics proficiencies identified in the Anytown math curriculum
2. To monitor mathematics instruction and make adjustments as needed to the Anytown mathematics curriculum
3. To prepare students for the state test math assessments in grades 4, 8, and 10

## Average Percent of Correct Responses

The district averages represent the average percent of correct responses for the grade level indicated. Individual school performances are presented in the accompanying charts.

An analysis of the average percent of correct responses shows slight increases in kindergarten and grades 1, 2, 3, and 5, and a slight decrease in grade 6. The content of the intermediate grade MASTERCRAFT math test was altered for the 2000–01 school year to increase the rigor and comprehensive nature of the exam, and the slight decrease may be a result of this change. Overall, elementary students averaged 72–91 percent correct responses on the MASTERCRAFT mathematics exam, indicating moderate to high levels of performance on this assessment, with declining percentages as students progress into the intermediate grades.

## Percent of Students Reaching Benchmarks

Further analysis of the MASTERCRAFT mathematics tests was done by setting benchmarks of percent of correct responses. This allows principals and teachers to analyze the results according to the number and percent of students who correctly completed answers to the MASTERCRAFT math tests. Reported below are the

| Year | Grade | District Average | Correct Responses |
|---|---|---|---|
| 1999–2000 | K | 16.3 | 90% |
| 2000–01 | K | 16.3 | 91% |
| 2001–02 | K | 16.5 | 91.8% |
| 1999–2000 | 1 | 21.8 | 91% |
| 2000–01 | 1 | 21.4 | 89% |
| 2001–02 | 1 | 21.7 | 90.4% |
| 1999–2000 | 2 | 26.3 | 88% |
| 2000–01 | 2 | 25.4 | 85% |
| 2001–02 | 2 | 25.7 | 85.7% |
| 1999–2000 | 3 | 25.8 | 78% |
| 2000–01 | 3 | 27.5 | 83% |
| 2001–02 | 3 | 27.8 | 84.3% |
| 1999–2000 | 5 | 31.6 | 79% |
| 2000–01 | 5 | 29.9 | 75% |
| 2001–02 | 5 | 30.68 | 76.7% |
| 1999–2000 | 6 | 30.7 | 77% |
| 2000–01 | 6 | 29.5 | 74% |
| 2001–02 | 6 | 29.1 | 72.9% |

benchmark results for 90, 80, 70, and 60 percent for each grade level tested. Results are based on the total percent of correct responses. For example, 43.5 percent of all students who took the MASTERCRAFT math in elementary school in 2002 produced a score between 90 and 100 percent correct.

### District Results 2002—Mathematics, K, 1, 2, 3, 5, 6

Total number of students tested = 5,190

| Benchmark band | Students who scored at benchmark |
|---|---|
| 90–100% | 43.5% |
| 80–89% | 25.0% |
| 70–79% | 15.2% |
| 60–69% | 8.7% |
| 59–0% | 7.6% |

## All Elementary Students in Tested Grades

| | 2001 | 2002 |
|---|---|---|
| 90% benchmark or above | 42% | 43.5% |
| 80% benchmark or above | 67% | 68.5% |
| 70% benchmark or above | 83% | 83.7% |
| 60% benchmark or above | 92% | 92.4% |

More than two-thirds (68.5%) of all elementary students who took MASTERCRAFT math produced a score at 80% accuracy or above. Forty-three percent (43.5%) of all elementary students who took MASTERCRAFT math produced a score at 90% accuracy or above.

## Item Response Analysis

The objectives for each MASTERCRAFT math test are presented to show the number of items devoted to each objective and the content of that objective. These MASTERCRAFT objectives match the curriculum objectives found in the Anytown mathematics curriculum guide. The MASTERCRAFT math test does not include an assessment for every curriculum objective because of the depth and complexity of the entire curriculum. Instead, MASTERCRAFT tests measure a sampling of objectives from the whole curriculum. See the attached reports of MASTERCRAFT math objectives tested in 2002.

The item response analysis shows each question on the MASTERCRAFT math test, the correct answer to that question, and the percent of students who answered each possible response. For example, the interpretation for the item below is that question 1 of the test had four possible responses. Of those choices, answer A was the correct answer. Ninety-three percent (93%) of the students who took the test gave A as their answer. Six percent gave B; one percent chose C. No student chose D as an answer.

| Q# | Answer | A | B | C | D |
|---|---|---|---|---|---|
| 1 | A | 93% | 6% | 1% | 0% |

One use of the item response analysis is to determine which questions are most often answered correctly. Further analysis shows questions where a high number of students chose a different answer. Anytown's curriculum coordinators will assist schools in analyzing item response reports and in making instructional adjustments based on these data.

# Appendix B
# Sample School Portfolio

**Achievement City Public Schools**
**State of the Schools—School Portfolio**
**2004–05**
**MASTERCRAFT[1]—Social Studies**

MASTERCRAFT is a software program that fosters the development of K–12 articulated curriculum goals that match national, state, and local standards and the development of local assessments to measure student learning. MASTERCRAFT software was put into use in Anytown for the first time in social studies during the 2004–05 school year.

The MASTERCRAFT social studies tests were created locally by selecting key social studies goals at each grade level and choosing test items that measure that goal. A multiple-choice format was used for the first administration of MASTERCRAFT social studies. This format matches the multiple-choice portion of the state assessment tests.

## Purposes of the MASTERCRAFT Social Studies Assessment

1. To give feedback to administrators, teachers, and students on levels of social studies proficiencies identified in the Anytown social studies curriculum

[1] MASTERCRAFT is a fictional program.

2. To monitor social studies instruction and make adjustments as needed in the Anytown curriculum
3. To prepare students for the state social studies assessments in grades 4, 8, and 10

## School Averages

The school averages represent the average percent of correct responses for the grade level indicated.

MASTERCRAFT—Social Studies
Percent of Correct Responses
**School Averages**

| YEAR | K | 1 | 2 | 3 | 4 | 5 | 6 |
|---|---|---|---|---|---|---|---|
| | | | | | | | |
| | | | | | | | |
| | | | | | | | |
| | | | | | | | |
| | | | | | | | |
| | | | | | | | |
| | | | | | | | |

### ANALYSIS

Write a short narrative that analyzes the results of the MASTERCRAFT social studies scores for the school.

# Appendix C
# Preparing for a Data Consultation

The data consultation is a process of collecting and analyzing data related to school improvement that culminates in a conference between the school leader and his or her supervisor.

**Purposes:**

1. To foster proven practices in instructional leadership related to providing focus and vision for the school (e.g., data-driven decision making, goal setting, and use of staff development to improve instruction)
2. To facilitate coaching and reflective dialogue between the principal and his or her supervisor
3. To analyze school data as they support the school improvement plan and professional development efforts

## I. Conduct a Thorough Examination of the State of the Schools Report

- Examine every section of the State of the Schools report or other collections of school data to look for information that relates directly to your school. Look for comparisons to previous years, to other schools, and to the district and state averages.
- Locate the data analysis guide and questions handout in the State of the Schools report under the portfolio section (see Figure 3.6, on p. 57). Use these questions as a guide for analyzing each piece of data from the report. Be prepared to answer these questions during the data consultation. Select those most relevant to your school as focus questions.

## II. Complete Basic Analysis Forms and Data Analysis Tools

• Use the forms found in the portfolio section of the State of the Schools report to help you begin to make sense of the data. The MAP worksheets are foundational to your data analysis work. Use these worksheets first. Next, you may want to develop your own worksheets or use worksheets from past analyses. A multiyear trend line graph for each subject area and grade level must be included in your analysis efforts.

## III. Prepare a Written Data Summary

### A. Just the Facts

• After reviewing all available data and preparing worksheets to assist you with your analysis, prepare a written data summary. Start with just the facts. Make a list of facts that summarizes the data.

**Example:** More than half of the students (52%) at grade 2 who took the SAT 9 reading test scored at or above the 50th percentile. This represents a 3% increase from the previous year.

• Put the data into words for readers who are unfamiliar with the analysis. Use words to describe what the numbers say.

### B. Big Ideas

• Write brief statements that are "big ideas" that you have gleaned from the data. These statements are not a summary of facts; they are an analysis or synthesis based on interpretation. Ask yourself: **What are the big ideas that came to me as I looked at all the data? What connections did I make?** Record your answers as your big ideas.

**Example:** Results from both the MAP mathematics test in grade 4 and the SAT 9 scores in grades 1–5 show that students are performing better in total mathematics over the past two years. However, computation scores have shown a slight decrease in the SAT 9 scores for students in grades 3–5. This trend has occurred for the past two years.

## IV. Develop Action Steps

• Write a few action steps suggested by the data. What will happen at your school as a result of understanding these data? These action steps should be based on your data analysis. Before considering implementing these steps, complete Section V below.

### V. Align Data with the School Improvement Plan and Action Steps

• Review your list of action steps to determine if they are big wheel or little wheel issues. Big wheel issues are the things you do that move you forward but take more time and development to make them happen. Big wheels are primary focus areas for your professional development and school improvement efforts. Little wheels are smaller, short-term items that you have to get done.
• Determine how your action steps match the goals in your school improvement plan. What, if any, changes may be needed in light of the new information you have from the data analysis? Be cautious about making rapid changes to the school improvement plan without sufficient data to support a course correction.

### VI. Review the Professional Development Plan

• Make connections between your school improvement and professional development plans that will occur at your school. How do the data support the need for further professional development in the areas you have chosen?
• How do the data confirm or deny the effectiveness of your school's professional development? Are the outcomes for students better as a result of the professional development? What data support this information?

### VII. Prepare the School Portfolio

• Prepare a portfolio that contains essential data adequate to discuss your school's progress in depth. The following list of items needs to be included in your portfolio. Feel free to innovate and add data specific to your school improvement and professional development efforts.

**A. Portfolio Contents** (organize these items in a manner that best fits you)

1. Data analysis
2. Just the facts summary
3. Big ideas statements
4. Action steps
5. Current school improvement plan
6. Current professional development plan or long-range plan
7. School demographic information

## B. Basic Worksheets

### 1. School's gains and losses

- Document that shows gains and losses from current and previous years for all subjects
- Document that shows upper two and lower two achievement levels for multiple years

### 2. Percentage of students at achievement levels

- Document that shows trend line graphs for all subjects over multiple years
- Document that shows upper two and lower two achievement levels for multiple years

### 3. State, district, and school comparisons

- Document that shows percentage of students at the upper two and lower two achievement levels as compared throughout the state, district, and school
- Document that shows state, district, and school comparisons over multiple years

### 4. Number of students at achievement levels

- Document that shows the number of students for all subjects over multiple years
- Document that shows the number of IEP students

### 5. Content Standards and Process Standards

- Document that shows all subjects and standards over multiple years

### 6. Disaggregated Groups

- Document that shows percentage and number of students for all subjects and achievement levels

## C. Items to Bring to the Data Consultation

1. Your school portfolio that includes:
   - a. Worksheets and analysis aids
   - b. Just the facts summary
   - c. Big ideas statements

   d. Action steps
2. Your current school improvement plan
3. Your current professional development plan that includes:
   a. Dates for all professional development activities
   b. Topics and descriptions of each activity
   c. Budget allocations
   d. Professional development evaluation tools and data to show high levels of evaluation

# Appendix D
# School Improvement Plan Overview

**School Improvement Plan—Page A**
**Overview**

**School**____________________________ **Principal** ____________________ **Date**________

| | | | | | |
|---|---|---|---|---|---|
| 7th Day Enrollment | 03–04___ | 04–05___ | 05–06___ | 06–07___ | 07–08___ |
| % Free/Reduced-Priced Lunch | 03–04___ | 04–05___ | 05–06___ | 06–07___ | 07–08___ |

Describe the primary focus of the school improvement efforts for the current school year.

Describe the primary focus of the school improvement efforts for the upcoming school year.

Briefly describe the process used to update the school improvement plan.

| No. | School Improvement Goals | State Standard Correlation Number(s) |
|---|---|---|
| I. | | |
| II. | | |
| III. | | |
| IV. | | |

## School Improvement Plan—Page B
## Goals and Strategies

School____________________________ Updated for school year____________________________

| No. | School Improvement Plan Goal (One goal per page.) | State Standard Correlation Number(s) |
|---|---|---|
| | | |

| No. | School Strategies | Narrative Evaluation of Strategy (How will you know if a strategy is working to accomplish objective?) |
|---|---|---|
| | | |
| | | |
| | | |
| | | |
| | | |

## School Improvement Plan—Page C
## Action Steps

**School:**
**Goal:**
**Strategy No. and Description:**

**Key: I = Initiated P = Progressing M = Met C = Canceled**

| Action Step # | I | P | M | C | Person Responsible | Action Steps to Implement Strategy: |
|---|---|---|---|---|---|---|
| | | | | | | *Anticipated completion date:* |
| | | | | | | *Anticipated completion date:* |
| | | | | | | *Anticipated completion date:* |
| | | | | | | *Anticipated completion date:* |
| | | | | | | *Anticipated completion date:* |
| | | | | | | *Anticipated completion date:* |
| | | | | | | *Anticipated completion date:* |
| | | | | | | *Anticipated completion date:* |
| | | | | | | *Anticipated completion date:* |
| | | | | | | *Anticipated completion date:* |

# Appendix E

# Questions and Answers About Displays of Student Work

**Q: Why are we so concerned about displaying student work?**
**A:** A display of student work conveys what is expected as a standard for good work. When both the criteria for good work and models of work that illustrate the criteria are displayed, the focus on meeting high standards becomes clear. Displays of student work are a way to communicate clear expectations for meeting high standards. The displays are powerful tools for communicating to students and adults how the standards look in a piece of authentic student work.

**Q: How does displaying student work help raise student achievement?**
**A:** Improved achievement happens when students meet high standards. Displays of student work model what meeting the standards looks like. This is only true if the standards for good work are discussed with students and student work is judged according to the specific criteria that meet the standard. It is not enough to simply post student work. To raise student achievement, students must know what the criteria for good work are and actively seek to apply the criteria to their own work. The more students seek to do work that meets high standards, the greater student achievement is. Displays of student work provide the models and visual images of what work that meets the standard looks like.

**Q: What does an effective display of student work include?**
**A:** An effective display includes several aspects. One is a label or some explanation of the assignment. This helps the observer to establish a frame of reference for examining the work. Another is a scoring guide or rubric. This valuable tool

provides the criteria by which student work is judged. The scoring guide is only as effective as the level of understanding by the student regarding what the scoring guide outlines as good work. Displays should be easily seen by students and adults. Placement of the work needs to be at a level that students can see in order for them to benefit from it. The display needs to showcase actual student products. Commercial materials such as teaching posters or charts may add color and content to the display, but unless they illustrate what good work looks like, little value is added. Good displays focus on what students know and can do. Good displays are neat and organized and include the following:

- Label or explanation of assignment
- Scoring guide or rubric
- Can easily be seen by students
- Showcase authentic student work
- Are neat and organized

**Q: Should grades be posted with the work?**
**A:** The purpose of posting student work is to show models of what work that meets a standard looks like. Therefore, more important than a grade is the clear expression of what the student did in the work that meets the criteria for good work. For example, if the criterion for good work in a mathematics assignment is to produce a written summary of the problem-solving process, the piece of student work displayed should clearly indicate how the student met that criterion. Writing comments on the work such as "Your summary statement was clear. I can easily follow the process you used" gives specific and useful feedback to the student. Attaching a scoring guide with a numerical assessment of how well the work met the criteria is also helpful. Specific feedback on student work far exceeds a letter grade in providing information to the learner that improves future performance.

**Q: Doesn't this take a lot of teacher time?**
**A:** Student displays of work take little time when teachers develop efficient procedures for posting work. One way to use displays as tools for learning is to delegate the display to students themselves. For example, students can write a brief description of the assignment for a label. Students can post a copy of the scoring guide and select work samples that illustrate the criteria on the scoring guide. Students can post the work in neat and organized ways. The act of displaying the work can be a learning activity if the teacher establishes the routines for making a display

and consistently teaches the rationale for displaying work. The display can also be posted by school volunteers.

One way to save time is to use the work that students normally do for the class rather than inventing work assignments just for display. A well-constructed display of student work takes far less time than bulletin boards created by the teacher for classroom decoration.

# Appendix F

# Examples of Weekly Messages

## *Mausbach Message*

**Elementary Principals** **April 8, 2004**

**Upcoming Events/ Deadlines**

**April 19th**
- Tech Mentors / Tech PD, 4:15-5:30, ERC

**April 20th**
- Mentor Celebration, 4:30-5:45, SVMS
- HOPE Awards, 7:00, LMS

**Team Meeting Agenda Items**

- Check in with school improvement plan and data
- Discuss field trip selection at their grade level
- Solicit input on any changes for the curriculum map

### Curriculum Items

1. **Elementary Field Trips**
   As you know, we have been investigating common field trips for students K–7. We have received feedback from teachers and visited several of the suggestions. The trips that have been designated for each grade level were picked because of their strong curricular match. Field trips that have been designated for next year are as follows:

| Grade | Field Trip | Curricular Focus |
|---|---|---|
| Kindergarten | Kaleidoscope | Literacy |
| 1st Grade | Wonderscope | Science and Social Studies |
| 2nd Grade | Martha Lafite (Colossal Fossil trip) | Science |
| 3rd Grade | Town Square | Social Studies |
| 4th Grade | Jefferson City and Earthworks | Science and Social Studies |
| | Liberty Symphony | Music |
| 5th Grade | Exchange City and | Social Studies |
| | HS Track & MS Transition | Physical Education |

*continued on Pg. 2*

***Mausbach Message*** Pg. 2

1. **MAP Test Pick-Up Date**
   MAP tests may be picked up at the ERC on Wednesday, April 14th. Please make sure that once the tests are in your building they are stored in a secured area. Give Barb a call if you have any questions regarding administration. Remember that this year, staff is not allowed to have posters hanging in the room with strategies, etc. even if they have been up all year. This is a change from last year's procedures.

2. **Speaking of MAP — SASI Changes for Pre-coding**
   As you know, we had some difficulty gathering the student data we needed in order to pre-code the MAP SIFs. Part of our problem was that demographic data are not in one location. In order to ensure that we have the correct information on students we will be putting all of the MAP fields (sped, LEP, FRL, in district less than a year, etc.) in SASI as part of the student record information. It will be great to have these fields accessible from SASI, but the important piece is making sure they are filled in properly for each and every student in your building. To help ensure that the fields are filled in correctly we are offering training for you and your secretaries this summer. It is critical that you attend this training so that secretaries can work throughout the summer on updating student records. Following is the training schedule. Please let me know if you cannot attend. Thanks for your help with this important issue.

   Elementary Principals and Secretaries — June 1, 9–11, HS classroom lab
   Secondary Principals and Secretaries — June 3, 9–11, HS classroom lab

## Human Resources

**Kindergarten Numbers**
Please send *accurate* numbers of kindergartners (this means actual students, not number of packets passed out) enrolled to Jim and Steve via e-mail ASAP. Thanks!

*continued on Pg. 3*

**Mausbach Message** Pg. 3

## Thought for the Week: Leadership: Scaffolding for Teachers

This week during our meeting we discussed the notion of scaffolding instruction. The concept of scaffolding (Bruner, 1975) is based on the work of Vygotsky, who proposed that with an adult's assistance, children could accomplish tasks that they ordinarily could not perform independently. Recently, I came across an article by John Maxwell that talked about getting staff to "play above their heads." Maxwell proposes that your job as a leader isn't to bring out the best in your people. Through words and example, your goal is to get them to play over their heads—to do things they normally couldn't do and achieve beyond their gifts and abilities. This idea of playing over their heads reminds me of what we are trying to do with kids when we scaffold instruction for students.

How do we scaffold for our staff? Maxwell asserts it begins with passion. In order to inspire staff, start with these guiding principles:

1. **The value of teamwork.**
   Impress upon your people that, if you're going to be successful, you're going to be successful together. One is too small of a number to achieve greatness. COLLABORATE.
2. **Each player's role.**
   You work together, but each person has a particular job to do—otherwise he or she would not be needed. Make sure each individual knows what he or she needs to do to add the most value to the team.
3. **The raising of the bar.**
   Don't allow your people to grow comfortable maintaining the status quo, even if they're doing a good job. Raise the bar. Set a new standard for excellence.
4. **The importance of a good attitude.**
   As the saying goes, one bad apple spoils the whole bunch. When that bad apple is a bad attitude, it can absolutely ruin your team.
5. **Hope and encouragement.**
   When you're winning, nothing hurts. But when you have a bad month (or test scores!), when a key player leaves for greener pastures, or when your industry as a whole is struggling, you have to be the one who encourages your people to look for the light at the end of the tunnel.
6. **The big picture.**
   It's easy to become so focused on the details of a particular task or assignment that you forget what you're ultimately working toward. Frequently remind your team how all the pieces of the puzzle fit together.

Take some time to reflect on these principles. I hope they inspire passion in you and that you come back from the break ready to help your staff continue to "play over their heads." Have a great spring break!

# MOONEY MEMO

**Focus**
**Follow-up**
**Finish**

**November 24, 2003** **Vol.10-12**

## Dates and Things

- A **huge THANK YOU** to all schools for the displays and activities during American Education Week. The displays at East Hills made me smile inside and out because I could see in the work and photos posted a focus not seen in the displays of "yesteryear." Thank you for doing this extra duty and for incorporating what you know about good work into this project. It left a good impression on the public eyes that viewed our classrooms. Nicely done!

- Congratulations to Melody, who was recognized at the MSTA Convention in St. Louis as the MSTA Administrator of the Year. She joins a distinguished list of St. Joseph educators who have been honored in this way. Our own Roberta currently serves as the CTA President, another example of how SJSD administrators step up to do the important work of guiding professional organizations.

- Walkthroughs are progressing with several elementary schools, and all middle school supervisory walkthroughs were completed before Thanksgiving. Our work thus far has been exceptionally productive thanks to the focus provided by each principal. Our conversations are deeper and more targeted to looking at the implementation of the school's school improvement and professional development plans. What a joy to be with you!

- The pins are here! You know, the ones you will use to record where each of your students is living according to your handy-dandy pin map. Your very own boxes of pins and the color key will be coming soon to a school near you via interschool mail. Please alert your mailroom staff to watch for them. This will be a good chance for you to say (so that others can hear), "Oh, gosh! The pins are here! Now I'll be able to work on that pin map for the central office. You know, we are all making these pin maps because we might have to know where school boundaries are located in case there is a school closing and redistricting. Well, at least the pins are here…"

*continued on Pg. 2*

MOONEY MEMO Pg. 2

- On Wednesday, Nov. 26th, Judith will be honored by her school at a special assembly at 8:30 a.m. This will be a special day for Judith and for her school family.
- Basketball season will kick off with the annual Basketball Jamboree next week. The girls begin playing at 3:30 p.m., Tuesday, Nov. 25, at the Civic Arena. The boys will begin playing around 7 p.m. Just give Vince, Melody, Steve, or me a call to let us know how many tickets you need.
- Gov. Holden will be in town next week to host an education roundtable at Missouri Western. The event is set for 2 p.m., Tuesday, Nov. 25 in the Spratt Multipurpose Building, Room 214. Our superintendent will be among the presenters, who include other educators as well as representatives of the business community.
- Thanks for your assistance in coordinating the meetings with faculty for the levy campaign and insurance information. Both activities are nearly completed for all schools. Your support and involvement make these things go smoothly.

| | |
|---|---|
| Nov. 26 | Early out for Thanksgiving break |
| Dec. 1 | Walkthrough at LHS —AM |
| Dec. 2 | PRINCIPAL MEETINGS — 8:00 a.m. HS, 10:30 a.m. — MS<br>1:30 p.m. - Elementary @ Lindbergh School |
| Dec. 3 | Late start for professional development |
| Dec. 4 | Walkthrough at Noyes — 9 a.m. |
| Dec. 8 | Board of education meeting<br>Study session 5:30: Counseling |
| Dec. 10 | Walkthrough at Pershing — AM |
| Dec. 11 | K–12 Principal meeting at TMC<br>PD topic: continuing our work with observing in classrooms |

PD and Look Fors

As professional development moves into the winter of the school year, it may be time for faculty to consider how what we are learning in professional development plays out in the daily bump and grind of teaching and learning. In other words, what would one reasonably look for in the classroom as a reflection of what is being learned through professional development? If there are no connections between PD and the real world of teaching, then the money invested in PD could just as well be spent on buying floor wax or a better brand of masking tape. The reason we have ongoing and focused professional development links directly to improvements in practice. It is not too soon to end your PD time with teachers by asking, "What would one reasonably look for in the classroom as a reflection of what we've learned today?" The answer to that question becomes the Look For, even if it is a preliminary one. The job of the principal is to look for the Look For and reward approximations of it in practice. It makes sense to have this discussion as a means of evaluating professional development effectiveness. It makes sense to link PD with school improvement. And it makes sense to engage faculty in identifying what to look for as a means of accountability for implementation. Brrrrr, I feel the chill of winter coming on — time to look for beginning levels of implementation!

*continued on Pg. 3*

MOONEY MEMO

Pg. 3

**A Matter of Principal**

**"Count your blessings; name them one by one…"**
These opening lines of a familiar Thanksgiving hymn convey the simple suggestion to step back from the cares of the world and take account of the things that are good and right. What is good and right in our work…our professional blessings? I challenge you to grab a pen and paper and make a quick list of at least three professional blessings in your working life. How specific is your list? The lyrics of "Count Your Blessings" encourage us to "name them one by one." Being specific narrows the focus. It's why the research on giving feedback and praise always reports the critical importance of specificity. Apply this to counting your professional blessings. Be specific about appreciating what is good about your work and those you work with. Narrow your focus by clearly identifying your professional blessings. Name them one by one so you can see the joy in doing good work. Identify the things that are praiseworthy so you can pass that specific feedback along to others. Then you will become a blessing to someone else. This Thanksgiving, I'm counting my personal and professional blessings.

# References


Atwell, N. (1987). *In the middle.* Portsmouth, NH: Heinemann.

Bernhardt, V. (2002). *The school portfolio toolkit.* Larchmont, NY: Eye on Education.

Blanchard, K., & Hodges, P. (2003). *The servant leader: Transforming your heart, head, hands, and habits.* Nashville, TN: J. Countryman.

Blasé, J., & Blasé, J. (1997). *The fire is back! Principals sharing school governance.* Thousands Oaks, CA: Corwin Press.

Blumberg, A. (1974). *Supervision and teachers: A private cold war.* Berkeley, CA: McCutchan.

Calkins, L. (1994). *The art of teaching writing.* Portsmouth, NH: Heinemann.

Champion, R. (2003). Taking measure: The innovation configuration. *NSDC Tools for Schools*, *2*(2), 69-70.

Cogan, M. L. (1973). *Clinical supervision.* Boston: Houghton Mifflin.

Collins, J. (2001). *Good to great.* New York: Harper Business.

Costa, A. L., & Garmston, R. (1985, February). Supervision for intelligent teaching. *Educational Leadership*, *42*(5), 70–80.

Costa, A. L., & Garmston, R. (2002). *Cognitive coaching: A foundation for renaissance schools* (2nd ed). Norwood, MA: Christopher-Gordon.

Council of Chief State School Officers. (1996). *Interstate school leaders licensure consortium: Standards for school leaders.* Washington, DC: Author.

Danielson, C. (1996). *Enhancing professional practice: A framework for teaching.* Alexandria, VA: Association for Supervision and Curriculum Development.

Danielson, C., & McGreal, T. (2000). *Teacher evaluation to enhance professional practice.* Alexandria, VA: Association for Supervision and Curriculum Development.

Darling-Hammond, L. (1997). *The right to learn.* San Francisco: Jossey-Bass.

Downey, C., Steffy, B., English, F., Frase, L., & Poston, W. (2004). *The three-minute classroom walk-through: Changing school supervisory practice one teacher at a time.* Thousand Oaks, CA: Corwin Press.

DuFour, R. (2004, May). What is a professional learning community? *Educational Leadership*, *61*(8), 6–11.

DuFour, R., & Eaker, R. (1998). *Professional learning communities at work.* Bloomington, IN: National Educational Service.

Easton, L. (2004). *Powerful designs for professional learning.* Oxford, OH: National Staff Development Council.

Evans, R. (1996). *The human side of school change.* San Francisco: Jossey-Bass.

Finnan, C., St. John, E., McCarthy, J., & Sloacek, S. (Eds.). (1995). *Accelerated schools in action: Lessons from the field*. Thousand Oaks, CA: Corwin Press.

Fletcher, R., & Portalupi, J. (2001). *Writing workshop: The essential guide*. Portsmouth, NH: Heinemann.

Fullan, M. G. (1996, February). Turning systematic thinking on its head. *Phi Delta Kappan, 77*(6), 421.

Fullan, M., & Stiegelbauer, S. (1991). *The new meaning of educational change*. New York: Teachers College Press.

Ginsberg, M. (2004). Classroom walkthroughs. In L. B. Easton (Ed.), *Powerful designs for professional learning*. Oxford, OH: NSDC.

Ginsberg, M. B., & Murphy, D. (2002, May). Walkthroughs open doors. *Educational Leadership, 59*(8), 34–36.

Glanz, J., & Sullivan, S. (2000). *Supervision in practice: 3 steps to improving teaching and learning*. Thousand Oaks, CA: Corwin Press.

Glickman, C. D. (1985). *Supervision of instruction: A developmental approach*. Boston: Allyn and Bacon.

Goldhammer, R. (1969). *Clinical supervision: Special methods for the supervision of teachers*. New York: Holt, Rinehart, & Winston.

Gould, J. S., & Gould, E. J. (1999). *Four square writing method*. Carthage, IL: Teaching and Learning Co.

Graves, D. (1983). *Writing: Teachers and children at work*. Portsmouth, NH: Heinemann.

Guskey, T. (2000). *Evaluating professional development*. Thousand Oaks, CA: Corwin Press.

Hall, G., & Hord, S. (2001). *Implementing change: Patterns, principles and potholes*. Boston, MA: Allyn and Bacon.

Harvey, S., & Goudvis, A. (2007). *Strategies that work: Teaching comprehension for understanding and engagement*. Portland, MA: Stenhouse.

Haycock, K. (1998, Summer). Good teaching matters…a lot. *The Education Trust*, 3(2), 3–14.

Heifetz, R. (1994). *Leadership without easy answers*. Cambridge, MA: Belknap Press of Harvard University.

Holcomb, E. (2004). *Getting excited about data*. (2nd ed). Thousand Oaks, CA: Corwin Press.

Hunter, M. (1986). The Hunter model of clinical supervision. In *A practical guide for instructional supervision: A tool for administrators and supervision*. Sacramento, CA: Curriculum and Instruction Leaders Committee, Association of California School Administrators.

Ingersoll, R. M. (2003, January 7). To close the gap, quality counts. *Education Week*, 7–18.

Jacobs, H. H. (2004). *Getting results with curriculum mapping*. Alexandria, VA: Association for Supervision and Curriculum Development.

Joyce, B., & Showers, B. (1982, October). The coaching of teaching. *Educational Leadership*, 40 (1), 4–10.

Joyce, B., & Showers, B. (2002). *Student achievement through staff development*. (3rd ed.). Alexandria, VA: Association for Supervision and Curriculum Development.

Joyce, B., Wolf, J., & Calhoun, E. (1993). *The self-renewing school*. Alexandria, VA: Association for Supervision and Curriculum Development.

Kannapel., P. J., & Clements, S. K. (with Taylor, D., & Hibpshman, T.). (2005, February). *Inside the black box of high-performing high-poverty schools: A report from the Prichard Committee for Academic Excellence*. Lexington, KY: Prichard Committee for Academic Excellence. Available: http://www.prichardcommittee.org.

Keene, E., & Zimmerman, S. (1997). *Mosaic of thought: Teaching comprehension in a reader's workshop*. Portsmouth, NH: Heinemann.

Knight, J. (2004, Winter). Instructional coaching. *StrateNotes, 13*(3). University of Kansas Center for Research on Learning.

Labovitz, G. H., Sang Chang, Y., & Rosansky, V. (1993). *Making quality work*. New York: Harper Business.

Lambert, L. (1998). *Building leadership capacity in schools*. Alexandria, VA: Association for Supervision and Curriculum Development.

Lindstrom, P., & Speck, M. (2004). *The principal as professional development leader*. Thousand Oaks, CA: Corwin Press.

Martin-Kniep, G. (2000). *Becoming a better teacher: Eight innovations that work.* Alexandria, VA: Association for Supervision and Curriculum Development.

Marzano, R. J. (2003). *What works in schools: Translating research into action.* Alexandria, VA: Association for Supervision and Curriculum Development.

Marzano, R., Pickering, D., & Pollock, J. (2001). *Classroom instruction that works.* Alexandria, VA: Association for Supervision and Curriculum Development.

Marzano, R., Waters, T., & McNulty, B. (2005). *School leadership that works: From research to results.* Alexandria, VA: Association for Supervision and Curriculum Development.

Miller, D. (2002). *Reading with meaning: Teaching comprehension in the primary grades*. Portland, MA: Stenhouse Publishers.

Moon, J. (2005). *Guide for busy academics, No. 4: Learning through reflection*. York, UK: The Higher Education Academy.

NAESP. (1997). *Proficiencies for principals.* (3rd ed.). Alexandria, VA: NAESP.

NSDC. (2001). *National Staff Development Council standards for staff development.* (Rev. ed). Oxford, OH: NSDC.

Pajak, E. (2000). *Approaches to clinical supervision: Alternatives for improving instruction*. Norwood, MA: Christopher Gordon Publishers.

Pearson, D., & Gallagher, M. C. (1983). The instruction of reading comprehension. *Contemporary Educational Psychology, 8*, 317–344.

Piaget, J. (1973). *The child and reality: Problems of genetic psychology*. New York: Grossman Publishers.

Reeves, D. B. (2006). *The learning leader: How to focus school improvement for better results.* Alexandria, VA: Association for Supervision and Curriculum Development.

Richardson, J. (2001, October/November).Seeing through new eyes: Walkthroughs offer new way to view schools. *NSDC Tools for Schools.*

Richardson, J. (2004, October/ November). Taking measure: Innovation configurations gauge the progress of a new initiative. *NSDC Tools for Schools, 8*(2), 1–6.

Rosenholtz, S. J. (1991). *Teacher's workplace: The social organization of schools*. New York: Teachers College Press.

Schmoker, M. (2004, February). Tipping point: From feckless reform to substantive instructional improvement. *Phi Delta Kappan*, *85*(6), 424–432.

Schmoker, M. (2006). *Results now: How we can achieve unprecedented improvement in teaching and learning.* Alexandria, VA: Association for Supervision and Curriculum Development.

Schmoker, M., & Marzano, R. (1999, March). Realizing the promise of standards-based education. *Educational Leadership*, *56*(6), 17–21.

Sergiovanni, T. (1992). *Moral leadership: Getting to the heart of school improvement.* San Francisco: Jossey-Bass.

Sergiovanni, T. (2000). *The lifeworld of leadership: Creating culture, community, and personal meaning in our schools.* San Francisco: Jossey-Bass.

Sergiovanni, T. (2007). *Rethinking leadership: A collection of articles.* (2nd ed.). Thousand Oaks, CA: Corwin Press.

Sizer, T. (1997). *Horace's school: Redesigning the American high school*. New York: Marine Books of Houghton Mifflin.

Smith, M. (2006). Convocation speech to St. Joseph School District at Missouri Theatre, St. Joseph, Missouri.

Strong, R., Silver, H., & Perini, M. (2001). *Teaching what matters most: Standards and strategies for raising student achievement.* Alexandria, VA: Association for Supervision and Curriculum Development.

Sweeney, D. (2003). *Learning along the way: Professional development by and for teachers.* Portland, ME: Stenhouse.

Tomlinson, C. (2000). *Leadership for differentiating schools and classrooms*. Alexandria, VA: Association for Supervision and Curriculum Development.

Wagner, T. (2004, October 27). The challenge of change leadership. *Education Week*, *24*(9), 40–41.

Wallace, R., Engel, D., & Mooney, J. (1997). *The learning school: A guide to vision-based leadership*. Thousand Oaks, CA: Corwin Press.

Wiggins, G., & McTighe, J. (1998). *Understanding by design*. Alexandria, VA: Association for Supervision and Curriculum Development.

Wise, A. (2004). Teaching teams: A 21st-century paradigm for organizing America's schools. *Education Week*, *24*(5), 43.

# Index

Note: Page numbers followed by *f* indicate figures.

# About the Authors

## Nancy J. Mooney

Nancy J. Mooney currently serves as an education consultant on the following topics: school improvement, school leadership, and communication arts. She has 20 years of experience as a school administrator. She has served as a K–12 supervisor of language arts, an elementary principal, and an executive director of teaching and learning. In her role as executive director, she supervised all aspects of teaching and learning, including curriculum development and supervising principals. Nancy pioneered the blueprint processes in St. Joseph, Missouri, which resulted in significant improvements in achievement and earned state honors for her district.

Nancy has been recognized by the U.S. Department of Education and the National Elementary Principal Association as the National Distinguished Principal from Missouri. She has received the following awards: IRA Administrator Literacy Award (Northwest Missouri Chapter), Phi Delta Kappa Educator of the Year Award, the Distinguished Service Award for Excellence in Education from Northwest Missouri State University, and the Missouri Early Childhood and Parent Education Distinguished Service Award. Nancy can be contacted via e-mail at njmooney@mac.com.

## Ann T. Mausbach

Ann T. Mausbach works as a central office administrator in charge of teaching and learning for a school district in the Midwest. She has served as an administrator for 14 years. Her administrative experience includes serving as a coordinator of staff development, a director of curriculum, and as an assistant superintendent for curriculum and instruction. By using the processes outlined in this book, Ann has been able to initiate and implement programs and practices that resulted in higher achievement. Ann can be contacted via e-mail at tamausbach@cox.net.

## Related ASCD Resources: School Improvement

At the time of publication, the following ASCD resources were available; for the most up-to-date information about ASCD resources, go to www.ascd.org. ASCD stock numbers are noted in parentheses.

### Audio

*Changing Schools Through Changing Leadership* by Kathy O'Neill (CD: #504387)

*Identifying Researched-Based Solutions for School Improvement* by Monica Martinez (Audiotape: #205069)

*Using What Works in Schools to Plan School Improvement* by John Brown (CD: #505098)

### Mixed Media

*Making School Improvement Happen with What Works in Schools: An ASCD Action Tool Set* by John L. Brown (three three-ring binders) (#705055)

*Schooling by Design: An ASCD Action Tool* (three-ring binder with 450 pages and a CD-ROM) (# 707039)

### Print Products

*Educational Leadership, February 2005, How Schools Improve* (Entire Issue #105032)

*Enhancing Student Achievement: A Framework for School Improvement* by Charlotte Danielson (#102109)

*The Learning Leader: How to Focus School Improvement for Better Results* by Douglas B. Reeves (#105151)

*Results Now: How We Can Achieve Unprecedented Improvements in Teaching and Learning* by Mike Schmoker (#106045)

*Schooling by Design: Mission, Action, and Achievement* by Grant Wiggins and Jay McTighe (#107018)

*What Works in Schools: Translating Research into Action* by Robert J. Marzano (#102271)

### Videos and DVDs

*Guiding School Improvement with Action Research Books-in-Action* (one video) (#400215)

*What Works in Schools* (three 35-minute programs on DVD with a 140-page facilitator's guide) (#603047)

For additional resources, visit us on the World Wide Web (http://www.ascd.org), send an e-mail message to member@ascd.org, call the ASCD Service Center (1-800-933-ASCD or 703-578-9600, then press 2), send a fax to 703-575-5400, or write to Information Services, ASCD, 1703 N. Beauregard St., Alexandria, VA 22311-1714 USA.